Cambridge Elements ≡

Elements in Ancient Egypt in Context
edited by
Gianluca Miniaci
University of Pisa
Juan Carlos Moreno García
CNRS, Paris
Anna Stevens
University of Cambridge and Monash University

CERAMIC PERSPECTIVES ON ANCIENT EGYPTIAN SOCIETY

Leslie Anne Warden
Roanoke College

CAMBRIDGE
UNIVERSITY PRESS

CAMBRIDGE
UNIVERSITY PRESS

University Printing House, Cambridge CB2 8BS, United Kingdom

One Liberty Plaza, 20th Floor, New York, NY 10006, USA

477 Williamstown Road, Port Melbourne, VIC 3207, Australia

314–321, 3rd Floor, Plot 3, Splendor Forum, Jasola District Centre,
New Delhi – 110025, India

79 Anson Road, #06–04/06, Singapore 079906

Cambridge University Press is part of the University of Cambridge.

It furthers the University's mission by disseminating knowledge in the pursuit of
education, learning, and research at the highest international levels of excellence.

www.cambridge.org
Information on this title: www.cambridge.org/9781108744133
DOI: 10.1017/9781108881487

© Leslie Anne Warden 2021

First published 2021

A catalogue record for this publication is available from the British Library.

ISBN 978-1-108-74413-3 Paperback
ISSN 2516-4813 (online)
ISSN 2516-4805 (print)

Ceramic Perspectives on Ancient Egyptian Society

Elements in Ancient Egypt in Context

DOI: 10.1017/9781108881487
First published online: May 2021

Leslie Anne Warden
Roanoke College

Author for correspondence: Leslie Anne Warden, warden@roanoke.edu

Abstract: This Element demonstrates how ceramics, a dataset that is more typically identified with chronology than social analysis, can forward the study of Egyptian society writ large. This Element argues that the sheer mass of ceramic material indicates the importance of pottery to Egyptian life. Ceramics form a crucial dataset with which Egyptology must critically engage, and which necessitate working with the Egyptian past using a more fluid theoretical toolkit. This Element will demonstrate how ceramics may be employed in social analyses through a focus on four broad areas of inquiry: regionalism; ties between province and state, elite and non-elite; domestic life; and the relationship of political change to social change. While the case studies largely come from the Old through Middle Kingdoms, the methods and questions may be applied to any period of Egyptian history.

Keywords: Egyptian society, Old Kingdom, Middle Kingdom, Egyptian economy, Pottery

ISBNs: 9781108744133 (PB), 9781108881487 (OC)
ISSNs: 2516-4813 (online), (online), 2516-4805 (print)

Contents

1 Ceramics as Dataset

Egyptian history is typically defined by an arc of pharaonic power. The terms we use for Egyptian history are inherently political terms following the rise and fall of the royal house and assigned by modern scholars. The omnipresence of royal power is dictated by the textual record and appears to accord nicely with the tombs and temples that have, until recently, dominated Egyptian archaeology (Manning, 2013: 61–62). Yet as Egyptian archaeology increasingly addresses ancient Egypt settlements (see Moeller, 2016) and our understanding of the material record becomes more careful and nuanced, it is evident that a history of the royal house is not synonymous with Egyptian social history.

The discipline of history leans on textual data, but for much of the ancient Egyptian past that dataset is extraordinarily limited. Expanding our understanding of Egyptian society and the players within it thus requires that we look, too, at the archaeological record. The Egyptian archaeological record is diverse and arguably dominated by ceramics.[1] There are more potsherds than mummies or stelae or statues; more even than lithics, or beads, or animal bones. To ground this statement in figures: during three weeks of excavation in three 5 m × 5 m units at the Old-Middle Kingdom settlement site of Kom el-Hisn in 2018, we netted 86,964 sherds weighing a total of 1,616 kg (1.78 US tons). To quantify it in another way: when we packed up the artifacts at the end of the season, we packed over 120 sacks of ceramics and only 4 sacks of nonceramic finds. While necropolis excavations yield fewer pots, pottery can still be prolific: for example, the Abusir tomb of Werkaure yielded at least 2,144 individual vessels (Arias Kytnarová, 2014: 71). Of course, ceramics are better preserved in the archaeological record than other containers, such as basketry, and many artifacts are lost to us through decay, reuse, or accident. Regardless, the abundance of the ceramic corpus at all sites, at all periods, is a direct indicator of two things: the fundamental nature of ceramics in ancient Egyptian lifeways and the critical need to incorporate ceramic data into social archaeological inquiry to further understanding of daily life, economy, and trade – among other activities.

However, the amount of ceramic material is not proportionate to its study; rather, its abundance is one of the greatest deterrents to proper recording, publication, and research. Study of the material requires a team of people led by qualified experts, presence of storage facilities, and access to labs. Ceramic study thus requires both short- and long-term visions for recording and analysis. This Element will illustrate the importance of ceramic analysis to forward a full

---

[1] Though there are nuanced differences between the terms *ceramic* and *pottery*, practical use in Egyptian archaeology uses both interchangeably, as shall I. (For example, *ceramicists* are also *pot people*.)

reconstruction of ancient Egyptian society, presenting research questions applicable to pots and sherds and methods that are being used to provide some answers. It is not a research text but rather a guide for how to think about ceramics and, indeed, about mundane artifacts in general. Common and repetitious artifacts allow one to deduce and analyze social norms. In pottery-producing societies, pots are used to perform fundamental tasks (cooking, trade and exchange, ritual). A society's production and use of pottery is motivated by choices made at the individual, local, regional, and state level, allowing archaeologists to apply ceramic data to a host of differently scaled social questions. This Element approaches ceramics not as individual objects of utility or beauty (indeed, most of them are quite unattractive), but rather as a composite dataset that provides interesting answers to social questions. Ceramic analysis, then, is not a niche avenue of analysis. Rather, it is fundamental to social archaeological work.

I come to write this Element because, after near twenty years of working with ceramics in the field, I have seen how differently ceramics are prized and handled by different projects. The range is great, with some projects doing but the barest recording of ceramics or assigning the task to untrained student labor, to other projects where a professional ceramicist oversees a team of individuals to sort, record, and analyze the material. Yet in all cases ceramics are fundamental to archaeology and key to so much social interpretation. By highlighting the value of ceramics as objects comprehensive and key to Egyptian history, more than simple chronological indicators, I hope to also forward an argument for ceramic research to be integral to and supported within all archaeological field projects.

1.1 Ceramic Research and Egyptian Archaeology

Ceramic analysis in Egypt was formalized relatively recently, marked in part by the publication of *An Introduction to Ancient Egyptian Pottery* (Arnold and Bourriau, 1993). Important work certainly predates this text – such as *Studien zur altägyptischen Keramik* (Arnold, 1981) and Petrie's far earlier (1901) pioneering work on ceramic seriation – but *An Introduction to Ancient Egyptian Pottery* offered standardized terminology for ceramic manufacture and materials, providing a language that could be applied broadly to Egyptian material. By highlighting the importance of manufacture and fabric, the text elevated these traits in the discourse. Thus, the field of Egyptian ceramics was born, mostly as a categorical, descriptive endeavor.

Study of archaeological ceramics was, in general, a late bloomer in archaeology across the globe. It was more delayed in Egyptian archaeology, most likely due to the high levels of preservation in the Egyptian material record. The drive to study potsherds is certainly dampened when one has statues, monuments, texts, and even minutia such as desiccated bread to analyze. Elsewhere in the world, where the historic and material records were not so robust, theoretical approaches to archaeology were key to moving from recording artifacts to understanding culture. For prehistorians, ceramic study was innovative at an earlier date. Material properties, identification and typology of ceramic wares and types, and scientific analyses were introduced to the archaeologist in Anna O. Shepard's *Ceramics for the Archaeologist* (1956), over thirty-five years before such topics would be distilled for an Egyptological audience. Prudence Rice's *Pottery Analysis* (1987) continued technical discussions of material and characterization while expanding into anthropological discussion of style, economics, distribution, and ethnography. *Pottery in Archaeology* by Clive Orton and colleagues (originally 1993, reprinted as Orton and Hughes, 2013) provided a practical handbook with the latest technologies used in ceramic study as well as a guide to establishing methods and workflows for field processing of sherds. For the budding ceramicist, these texts provide fundamental groundwork for *how* to think about pottery.

In Egyptian archaeology, ceramic analysis ca. 2021 AD is quite active. Excavation monographs commonly dedicate chapters to the pottery (e.g., Raue, 2018b; Arias Kytnarová, 2014; Köhler, 2014a; Arnold, 1988a, 1988b). Alternately, some sites offer monographs dedicated to ceramic finds that are forward understandings of a site's chronology and can include theoretical interpretation (e.g., Bourriau and Gallorini, 2016; Rzeuska, 2006). Egyptian ceramicists gather at conferences to discuss their material and publish the proceedings (e.g., Bader et al., 2016; Bader and Ownby, 2013; Rzueksa and Wodzińska, 2009). Handbooks present guides to the ceramic corpora of specific periods (e.g., Schiestl and Seiler, 2012a; Wodzińska, 2009). Two stand-alone journals are dedicated to Egyptian ceramic research, both published by the Institut français d'archéologie orientale du Caire: *Cahiers de la céramique égyptienne* and *Bulletin de liaison de la céramique égyptienne* (also called *Bulletin de la céramique égyptienne*). Egyptian ceramic research is also published in broader archaeology journals and edited books.

Egyptian ceramic studies to-date yield excellent and broadly published research. But we can go further. Egyptian history specifically is made richer and more multidimensional by applying ceramic material to social questions – in other words, by viewing ceramics as data and working with them within a theoretical framework, building upon the work that has come before. Integrating ceramic research into social historical and social archaeological research, however, means ceramic data need to be put in conversation with all other types of information and specialists. This presents two additional challenges. The first is integrating ceramics firmly into all fieldwork. As will become apparent through this Element, many of the social analyses require quantification and careful recording of the sherds. Others require lab analyses. Both necessitate time and labor during a field season and afterward. Fundamental to this is more ceramicists! Ceramicists can work with excavation directors (and vice versa) early in a project's creation in order to create appropriate social research questions, plan for ceramic teams, and build them into research programs from the very beginning. These conversations, of course, require that all parties understand the values and outcomes of ceramic research to social archaeology. This brings us to the second challenge: ceramic work must be presented to a broader audience than just ceramicists to best impact reconstructions of Egyptian society. We can address a broader audience as well by turning ceramics on their head, placing the material second to the social questions we choose to address. This Element addresses those goals by highlighting ceramic case studies that forward social analyses, with the aim of addressing archaeologists, students, and the general public to showcase the value of these humble materials.

1.2 Studying Ceramics: Practical Concerns

Ceramic research can be assembled from primary data collected in publications, but the quantity and range of material varies widely between texts. Museums are another locus for ceramic data, though they rarely hold pottery fully representative of archaeological contexts. Active archaeological work provides the best opportunity to build a statistically relevant dataset that can provide a foundation of testable hypotheses. Ceramic research thus needs to be integrated into field programs. The director and ceramicist(s) must have clear understanding of the project's research questions and aims in order to build the necessary team and plan a suitable methodology, while respecting the project's budget.

The first step to identifying methodology is to determine the type of project. Ceramic preservation varies by project and site, meaning that no one methodology suits every project and not all questions can be answered by every corpus. Material will be dependent on archaeological project type (excavation or survey) and the type of site (settlement or cemetery). All things being equal, pottery from stratified excavation contexts can answer more detailed questions than pottery collected during archaeological surveys as it comes from more secure contexts allowing for diachronic analysis. Excavation will also tend to yield more ceramics. Surveys, though, are far from unimportant. Archaeological surveys allow for the discussion of broad landscape use, variation, and change over time; survey ceramics provide important indicators of chronology and function. Surveys tend to yield fewer ceramics, potentially eroded, as all finds come from the surface.

It is also important to recognize the type of site at which you are working and the resultant variation in ceramic preservation. The ceramic record at settlements and cemeteries is the result of different activities and depositional processes; the ceramics will differ by type of site and will allow for different questions to be answered (Bourriau, 1986–87). Pottery from tombs is more likely to be intact as they were part of an intentional deposition. The settlement record is full of sherds, rather than complete vessels, as most settlement deposits are dumps or fills. The vessels must either be reconstructed or the sherds recorded and analyzed in manners that account for their fragmentary state (Bader, 2016, 2010; Orton and Hughes, 2013). Sherds offer an additional challenge as one cannot always be certain of the type or size of the original vessel; accordingly, many of our published ceramic corpora focus on documenting complete vessels found in tomb contexts (e.g., Rzeuska, 2006; Reisner and Smith, 1955).

Before going into the field, one must establish research questions; these inform both methodology and sampling method. For example: at Elephantine, I am interested in cooking patterns and the relationship between wares in an assemblage; data on blackening patterns and body sherds will aid understanding both of those issues. Research questions should be established by the ceramicist in conversation with the director. Both people bring important perspectives to the table. The director understands the overall vision of the project; they will inevitably have research questions that they hope the ceramicist will help answer. The ceramicist as a specialist knows their material thoroughly; by understanding pottery they will understand what it might be able to say. Both will also have an understanding of the practical realities of processing and storage and what one might do within those limitations. Good questions come from director and ceramicist working together. Strong questions also arise from collaboration across all the team members of the excavation, feeding multivariate datasets into complex reconstructions of ancient activities.

When it comes to research questions, the first and most fundamental question that a ceramicist will be asked is to date the deposits and, by extension, the site. It is common to assign a date to finds, from architecture to human remains, according to the ceramics with which they were found. Pottery is the cheapest means of archaeological dating. As pottery deposition can occur over long stretches of time, the date of the pottery found within a building might ultimately not accord with the original date of the building. Thus, ceramic dating should always be used as pottery dates can indicate long periods of primary or secondary use

Pottery may be dated by the change in style in a vessel type over time, something that the reader can likely intuit from their personal ceramics. My own American kitchen yields its best example from my mug collection, including a late 1980's mug (small, decorated with a cartoon Garfield) and a late 2000's mug (huge, decorated with pumpkins, with a Starbucks label on the bottom that I try to ignore). These vessels have styles that reflect their production in different periods. Both size and decoration have changed over time, indicating change in consumption patterns and consumer relationships. Of course, dating is made more complex in that two stylistically different vessels continue in actual use in 2020, reminding us that ceramics actually bear two dates: the vessel's date of manufacture and the date of its final use and deposition.

Dating pottery requires identifying specific ceramic types, understand the types' change over time, and placing the change within your broader corpus. Not all sherds yield dates and so chronological study does not work with the bulk of the material, though of course one must sort all the material in order to identify chronologically indicative sherds. W. M. Flinders Petrie first documented the utility of stylistic change in archaeological dating and the seriation method by which depositional dates might be determined in his study of predynastic vessels (Petrie, 1901). While exact methods have changed in the intervening 100 years, the theory behind seriation remains essentially the same. In cases where the context of the vessel is not clear, such as with archaeological surveys, vessel types are sometimes dated through equation to a like type from another site, preferably nearby, based on morphological attributes. Such dating by parallel can cause conflation in dating, creating a uniform chronology between multiple sites and eradicating any time lag or differentiation in the use of a type. Accordingly, paralleling is best taken as providing only *potential* dates; certain dates only arise through site-specific dating techniques such as stratigraphy, seriation, or assemblage dating.

The bulk of Egyptian ceramic studies have focused on chronology. But chronology is the beginning, not the end, of ceramic analysis, and chronology will be minimized in this Element. Instead, we will concentrate on functional and social analyses, which must be conducted at entirely different scales from chronological analysis. Functional analyses can be small-scale, limited to a single type (for example, Hendrickx et al., 2002) or even an individual pot; they require detailed knowledge of form, material, contents (when possible), and archaeological context. We can determine the life history of an individual vessel from manufacture to final deposition. Functional analyses thus provide a window into specific use, whether individual to a single vessel or a single type, allowing us to determine cultural practice at the level of small-scale, repeated action (see also Bader and Ownby, 2013).

"Social analyses," on the other hand, is a phrase I use here to reflect analyses aimed at reconstructing activities that reflect larger social and institutional relationships within a site and across the country. Such studies can be focused on a carefully limited dataset, sometimes as small as one vessel, particularly when the question at hand is reconstruction of elite trade networks (e.g., Hartung, 2001; Bourriau, 1996). Alternately, ceramic social analyses might strive to reconstruct statewide networks and social practices. Such analyses require a large dataset spanning some space – whether multiple locations within a site or several sites. The required scale means that the ceramics employed best come from multiple excavations or, in some cases, a single large excavation. The data will have been processed by many different ceramicists using many different methodologies, presenting a patchwork of data inevitably including some inconsistencies in terminology and recording.

1.3 The Structure of This Element

This Element is structured around questions about ancient Egyptian society. I will generally limit discussion to ceramics from the Old-Middle Kingdoms (ca. 2700–1650 BC, following Shaw, 2000; Table 1). This choice is one made based on my specialization and familiarity, *not* because interesting and important ceramic work cannot be found from other periods of Egyptian history. I shall front the social questions and make those questions central to our discussions so they may provide food for thought for other points in Egyptian history.

This Element begins by using the Pharaonic state as a reference and seeking to identify diversity under that umbrella. Section 2 approaches the relationship of state and province, treating ceramics as economic indicators for who held economic oversight and power. Different analyses of vessel morphology and volume show how one might approach the question of unification and standardization, highlighting regional difference and local or even individual agency. Section 3 investigates regionalism and identity through the lens of ceramic production, which was regional or even local, taking this to suggest that local identities and economic activities were also locally grounded. Section 4 highlights the challenges in applying the ceramic record to questions of dating, exploring the ties between political and social change. When we study ceramics as indicators of social change, rather than as a time marker in a political/historical chronology, the continuity of the Egyptian lived experience and the agency of Egyptian cities and localities to make bottom-up change becomes

Table 1 Chronology of Egypt to the end of the Middle Kingdom (after Shaw, 2000: 479–81)

Predynastic Period		ca. 5300–3000 BC
Maadi Cultural Complex (Lower Egypt)	ca. 4000–3200 BC	
Badarian Period (Upper Egypt)	ca. 4400–4000 BC	
Naqada I Period (Upper Egypt)	ca. 4000–3500 BC	
Naqada II Period (Upper Egypt)	ca. 3500–3200 BC	
Naqada III/Dynasty 0 (all Egypt)	ca. 3200–3000 BC	
Early Dynastic Period		**ca. 3000–2686 BC**
Dynasty 1	ca. 3000–2890 BC	
Dynasty 2	2890–2686 BC	
Old Kingdom		**2686–2125 BC**
Dynasty 3	2686–2613 BC	
Dynasty 4	2613–2494 BC	
Dynasty 5	2494–2345 BC	
Dynasty 6	2345–2181 BC	
Dynasty 7/8	2181–2160 BC	
First Intermediate Period		**2160–2055 BC**
Dynasties 9 & 10	2160–2025 BC	
Dynasty 11	2125–2055 BC	
Middle Kingdom		**2055–1650 BC**
Dynasty 11	2055–1985 BC	
Dynasty 12	1985–1773 BC	
Dynasty 13	1773–1650 BC	

apparent. Section 5 problemizes the population's lived experiences, investigating ethnic identity and household practice. The resultant picture of Egyptian society shows an Egypt composed of local individuals and diverse power networks, where identity was more locally crafted than monolithic. Case studies will come from throughout Egypt (Figure 1). For those readers less familiar with ceramic or archaeological terminology, a short Glossary is included at the end.

Sections are arranged from the public (economy, regionalism and state control, chronology and cultural change) to the private (ethnicity and domestic life). To an extent, the questions are also arranged by scale. Thus, the data required for addressing regionalism and state control, as well as economy, must

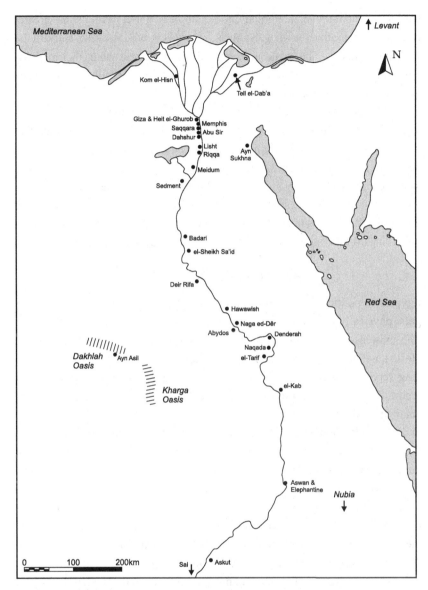

Figure 1 Map of Egypt and Lower Nubia with sites discussed in text.
(drawn by David S. Anderson)

come from multiple sites across the country. Comparison allows investigation into how sites and regions might have been networked together. Alternately, questions of ethnicity and private life might be answered with the material from one site, perhaps even just from one house. Of course, even then comparative data is useful and helps create a context in which to understand one's finds. It is hard to talk about Nubian ethnicity, for example, without having some greater idea and comparative for what "Nubian" material culture looks like. But still the division remains. The scale of one's data, combined with the methods employed, will in part determine how one can think about the data and the questions that might be asked.

Functional and social analyses of ceramics present possibilities for reconstructing ancient Egyptian society from its bottom up, rather than viewing the Egyptian masses through the necessarily limited lens of elite text and art. Many questions about Egyptian social organization, identity, and domestic life – to list but a few – await ceramicists for study and answer. I hope this Element challenges how you think about ceramics in specific and, by extension, all things utilitarian and mundane. The lived human experience can be encapsulated by the fundamental, ugly things we use and those basic things we throw away.

2 Integration of State and Province

Egypt as a political entity was a unified state imagined, in the *sema-tawy*, as parts physically united tied around the person of the king (Robins, 2000: 18). The existence of the king defined the existence of the state (Trigger, 1993: 10–13), with the royal house providing conceptual, ideological unity. Under the king served a number of central bureaucrats forming an administrative hierarchy. Their titles are often poorly linked with the actual responsibilities entailed, with much flux in the titles occuring over the millennia-and-a-half under consideration here. These individuals had wealth, allowing them to build the well-decorated stone tombs that survive today that form substantial part of our information about Egyptian society. Elite members of the royal administration served as intermediary individuals, owning land that was worked by members from lower classes and collecting goods from those same individuals (Baines, 2009–10: 117–44; Moreno García, 2001). Patronage relationships tied the elite to lower classes (Campagno, 2014; Warden, 2014; Moreno García, 2013), of whom we have very little direct knowledge.

It is the elite classes that scholars most often treat as the standard bearers of Egyptian culture. The artistic evidence from elite Memphite tombs routinely shows estates farmed by often unnamed individuals who would certainly seem to be reliant upon the work their elite patron provides. These elite individuals owned land throughout the country that was farmed and otherwise maintained by provincial, lower-class individuals. The elite would have collected goods from those same individuals (Baines, 2009–10: 117–44; Moreno García, 2001). As for the base of the hierarchy – small-scale and/or non-landholding farmers, bakers, brewers, potters, butchers, weavers, and the like – these individuals are largely invisible in text and art. Subsequently, they are largely absent from modern reconstructions of Egyptian society unless in investigations of daily life (Moreno García, 2017; Szpakowska, 2008). Yet defining Egyptian culture solely by its upper rungs is a limited perspective, especially as it is unclear how much the royal house was involved in provincial life. While the royal house and, by extension, its administration provided the conceptual and ideological unity necessary to define the Egyptian state, its scale and involvement in the organization of local institutions and activities is less certain. A key question here is how the state and provinces were integrated and how much provincial autonomy existed. Low integration would open space for provincial subcultures to flourish and would present an Egyptian society where the opportunity existed for individual agency.

Considering the role and potential agency of the non-elite in Egyptian society, rather than relying on elite state control as an explanatory mechanism, requires that one investigate fundamental social systems such as the economy. It also requires new datasets, as most text and monuments, particularly in the Old Kingdom, are created by the elite for an elite, often Memphite, audience and of necessity present a world view in which they dominate. The question then at hand is: how do ceramics allow us to approach cultural and economic integration? Ceramics' large dataset provides part of the key. All classes of Egyptian society deposited the pottery found in the archaeological record. Vessels were generally used by all socioeconomic classes in similar ways, though occasionally the elite had access to special types and wares (for example, Allen, 1998), and local types existed (see Section 3.3–3.4). Repetition and commonality in the ceramic record speaks of the routine and daily rather than the elite and the exceptional, thus providing the potential to analyze systems and large-scale integration.

2.1 Theories and Methods

The ceramic case studies highlighted in this section partly build upon typological study, focusing on the recording of the appearance and distribution of different ceramic types. Looking at presence, absence, and variable use of ceramic types by context helps expose relationships between socioeconomic classes within a given site. The second half of this section is built upon standardization studies, which arise out of anthropological archaeology's investigation of traditional craft production where no external measuring device is used to enforce exactitude. Measuring variation and identifying standardized manufacture in these circumstances requires the Weber fraction. The Weber fraction denotes the level of variation that the human senses can identify between objects (Eerkens and Bettinger, 2001: 494–95). That variation can be measured in archaeological assemblages and assessed for standardization in part by comparing to ethnoarchaeological findings (Eerkens and Bettinger, 2001; Eerkens, 2000; Longacre, 1999).

Ethnoarchaeology, the studying of living populations to develop models of how past activities *might* have occurred, provides an interpretative middle ground allowing archaeologists to work through ways in which human activity and social relationships can be decoded from material culture. Important ethnoarchaeological studies of modern Egyptian potters have been conducted that provide some models of production (e.g., Köhler, 1996; Nicholson and Patterson, 1985, 1989–90). As ethnoarchaeology provides models, not analogs, it can also be fruitful to look at ethnoarchaeological research conducted in other parts of the world (e.g., Skibo, 2013; Longacre, 1999, 1985). These latter studies are particularly crucial for understanding standardization.

Standardization studies differ from typological studies in that they require larger sample sizes to yield reliable statistical findings. Certainly, this is no great limitation in the Egyptian archaeological record, where some types are incredibly numerous in the ceramic corpora. Such is particularly true of utilitarian wares. Produced in huge quantities by large numbers of potters, utilitarian wares dominated Egyptian life and defined Egyptian activities. Their commonality and their repetition across different sites allow for the necessary inter- and intra-site comparison. However, even fine wares such as the Old Kingdom Meidum bowl (see Figure 2), were produced in great numbers and are thus suitable for standardization analyses as long as the relevant attribute data are collected during fieldwork.

2.2 Cultural Integration

We begin by investigating the relationships between classes within ancient Egyptian society. Defining social classes is itself a tricky business (see Richards, 2005: 13–18); we shall take *class* to indicate individual groups of similar wealth and status. Identification of an object as having been related to individuals of a given class rests strongly on the architecture of where it was found and, to a lesser extent, the archaeological assemblage to which it relates. For example, when found in a large house together with royal sealings, one can assume the ceramics were used by the elite. When found in a simple pit burial with no art or small objects, the ceramics can be treated as having been deposited by non-elite individuals. Often, though not always, the Egyptians clustered elite and non-elite houses and graves into the same areas. Thus, the relationship between classes is in part embodied within the site's landscape (Richards, 2005: 50–64, 173–80).

Lower class archaeological assemblages are, by definition, smaller and less complex than those created by their elite contemporaries. However, both elite

Figure 2 Old Kingdom Meidum Bowl. Rim diameter 21 cm, height 9.2 cm. (Metropolitan Museum of Art photo of their object 28.2.8; image used under CC0 1.0 license)

and non-elite ceramic assemblages commonly include the same ceramic repertoire. In general, elite status appears to have been marked not by use of different ceramic vessels, but by an increased number of those vessels and access to vessels of metal or stone (Arias Kytnarová et al., 2019; Odler, 2017).

Interesting, not only did the elite and non-elite use the same types of vessels, but broadly speaking the types of pottery made during the Old and Middle Kingdoms are recognizable at sites throughout Upper and Lower Egypt (for example, see Schiestl and Seiler, 2012a). The Egyptian ceramic corpus unifies in the late Predynastic Period, with the same ceramic types then being produced throughout the Egyptian Nile Valley (Köhler et al., 2011). The unification of the ceramic corpus occurs *before* political unification, undirected by a royal power. The king might have defined the ideology of Egyptian statehood, but "Egyptian-ness" as apparent in the objects people used and the way things were built was not directed by the royal house. The pots' general similarity further suggests that all potters were trained in the same basic manufacturing skills: coil- and slab-building, firing in a simple updraught kiln, and use of a simple low wheel. Production of vessels was not reliant upon household production. Rather, it seems to have fallen to full-time potters, who are apparent in the Egyptian archaeological record at least from the Early Dynastic Period (Köhler, 1997). By the Old Kingdom, it seems likely that specialist potters manufactured the vast majority of vessels employed by all classes of Egyptian society (Warden, 2011). The industry was not, however, centrally organized and variation within vessels and production existed (Warden,

2011). Rather, we know potters to have operated under the purview of elite estates and royal mortuary institutions; it is likely other potters worked attached to temples while still others could have been independently managed. Our understanding of the control and management of ceramic production exists only as a general picture; clearer resolution requires further excavations of pottery workshops and their surrounding settlements and institutions (e.g., Soukiassian et al., 1990). If most potters were specialists, then by extension both elite and non-elite individuals likely had access to the wares of specialist potters as we know both groups of people were regularly consuming pottery. Accordingly, the ceramic industry would have provided a regular point of cultural integration of the elite and non-elite, though one with complexities remaining to further puzzle out.

One notable vessel type for a discussion of integration is a bowl with recurved rim and white slip on both interior and exterior surfaces, given it the type code "CD7" by the ceramicist who first identified it (Wodzińska, 2006: Figure 3). In morphology and size, it mirrors a much more common form called the "Meidum bowl" that appears throughout Egypt during the Old Kingdom (Figure 2). However, Meidum bowls are identifiable through their red slip and glossy burnishing. CD7, with its white slip, is rare in the Old Kingdom ceramic corpus, being known exclusively at Heit el-Ghurob, the city that housed the labor that built the Giza Pyramids, and at Sheikh Said, a mining site in Middle Egypt (Vereecken, 2011; Wodzińska, 2007: 299–300; 2006). The appearance of CD7 at sites that are dedicated to royal building projects links it to government-sponsored production and use, perhaps as part of royal provisioning of labor forces. CD7 documents a small-scale integration of state activities across Egypt through government worksites. Interestingly, the limited occurrence of CD7 in

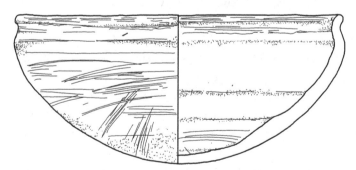

Figure 3 Bowl CD7. Morphologically, the vessel parallels the well-known Meidum bowl (see Figure 2); however, it is different in surface treatment. (Wodzińska, 2007: fig. 11.21; copyright 2020 by Ancient Egypt Research Associates)

the Egyptian ceramic record suggests that the practice of direct government payments for labor was similarly limited.

CD7's selective appearance at Old Kingdom sites is the exception that emphasizes the rule: ceramics were part of a cultural core of material to which all individuals had access. The similarity in ceramic repertoire highlights a consistency of cooking practices, use of basic commodities such as bread and beer, and access to similar ritual for all classes, making these factors basic markers of "Egyptian-ness" during the third and early second millennia BC.

2.3 Socioeconomic Integration

The social integration between these two communities, the members of the royal bureaucracy and the non- (or sub-) elite, can be forwarded by focusing on specific vessel types. The most useful ceramic types for this question will be those that are abundant, repeated many times within the ceramic corpora. Similarity and repetition within a site, as well as between sites, allows for analysis of possible points of contact or cultural likeness. The distribution and frequency of common types help build an understanding of function which can strengthen arguments for cross-class relationships.

Cemetery data, more broadly excavated and published than that from Egyptian settlements, begins our exploration of the relationships between elite and non-elite at cemetery sites. When working with cemetery ceramics, it is important to remember that artifacts deposited in different places in the tomb might have been deposited at different times, by different individuals, for different purposes. Thus, it is more accurate to divide the cemetery assemblage into three parts mirroring these divisions. *Funeral pottery* was placed in the tomb shaft with the rubble blocking the burial, likely by funeral attendees. *Cultic pottery* was used and deposited in the cult spaces (mortuary temple or cult chapel), in some cases long after the original internment. *Burial pottery* was placed in the actual burial for use by the deceased in the afterlife (Rzeuska, 2006: 430). Division allows us to speak more confidently of pottery function and social implications of that use.

The royal cemetery of Meidum provides one example. The most elite Meidum tomb was, of course, the Fourth Dynasty pyramid of Snefru (ca. 2600 BC) for which the site is primarily known. Next in rank were the owners of the mastabas built in a line to the north of the pyramid and contemporary to it, who served in Snefru's bureaucracy (Petrie, 1892; Petrie et al., 1910). The lowest class represented at this royal cemetery are sub- or non-elite individuals – their specific status is unclear, though their dependent position is evident – buried in shaft burials with no extant superstructure (Warden, 2013: 230–32). These small shaft tombs were the most common burial type at the site, largely grouped in two clusters between the mastabas of the northern cemetery. Several of the elite tombs had been plundered in antiquity, though the tomb robbers typically left the pottery behind as valueless and uninteresting to them. The sub-/non-elite tombs, on the other hand, were often found intact.

Unsurprisingly, elite tomb owners at Meidum employed a larger number of ceramic vessels than the owners of the small shaft tombs. Both communities had funeral and burial pottery. The cultic assemblage for both the king and elite individuals at Meidum was dominated by miniature vessels (Figure 4). Miniature vessels, appearing first in Dynasty 4, are typically under 10 cm in height and were produced not to hold food but rather to extend and stand in for ritual action (Allen, 2006: 21–22). The cultic importance of miniature vessels is clear, in large part due to their prominence in royal mortuary temples and tomb chapels throughout the Memphite necropolis beginning in the reign of Snefru (Allen, 2006: 22; Marchand and Baud, 1996: 269–84; Bárta, 1995a; Faltings, 1989: 137, 142, 153, Abb. 3, 7). They were used to mimic offerings given to the dead by the living. Their abundance in elite settings suggests that the cult was regularly repeated, signaling the living's ongoing devotion and maintenance of the deceased's spirit. Cultic pottery, however, is entirely absent for the sub-/non-elite tomb owners. If their souls were the

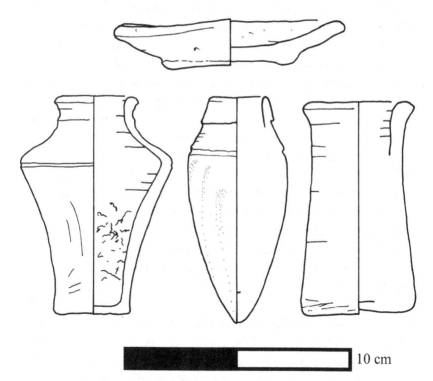

10 cm

Figure 4 Miniature vessels from Meidum, Dynasty 4. (drawn by author)

recipients of food or devotion, its practice is not evident in the archaeological record.

Elite individuals had access to cultic pottery, and therefore to cultic activities, unattainable to the lower ranking individuals buried nearby. Yet elite and sub-/ non-elite individuals had a similar funeral pottery assemblage. In both cases, the funeral pottery was dominated by the same miniature vessels also found in the elite cultic assemblages. The meanings and purposes of the vessels changed in their new location. In both mastabas and shaft tombs, miniature vessels were found placed intermittently within the shaft fill. They must have been placed there by the funeral attendees during the closure of the burial; their common presence strongly suggests that participants in elite and sub-/non-elite funerals used these pieces of material culture to enact the same or similar ceremonies and rituals at burial (Warden, 2013). Though the vessels suggest that these rituals involved the idea of a food offering, the actual ritual itself need not have been the same as that in regular cult practice. Their deposition was different, the result of a different set of practices. It is unclear if Snefru employed similar funeral rituals as the filling of the pyramid shaft is unknown. The dominance of miniature vessels is unlikely to indicate a simple "economization" of the offering cult (Bárta, 1995a: 18) as this vessel type crossed barriers of ritual (funeral and cult) and class (elite and non-elite). Instead, it would seem to mark aspects of funeral practice that incorporated multiple socioeconomic communities.

If Egyptian funerary ritual was similar across classes, it seems accordingly likely that all nonroyal Egyptians had access to the same religious ideology and the same afterlife (see further Hays, 2011). At the moment of internment, social division shrank, bringing us to a core cultural concept, a place of "Egyptian-ness" that was accessible to all individuals buried at Meidum.

One interesting point: miniature vessels had been treated as a largely mortu-ary phenomenon limited to the Memphite necropolis. This would suggest that they were somehow special to the cult of the royal house, its administration, and the sub-elite related to it. However, recent publication of miniature vessels from Elephantine Island challenges this assumption (Raue, 2018b: 186, 208–09, 224, Abb. 84). Burgeoning work at Egyptian settlements provides future opportun-ities to test the ceramic assemblage for points of integration between the mortuary and domestic spheres. Clearly, this vessel type has not yielded its final analysis.

2.4 State Dominance and Economic Integration

How well-integrated was state power into the landscape of the provinces? Textual evidence, via nonroyal titulary, presents a royal administration that was in some sense centralized, with national offices such as vizier (Strudwick, 1985: 321–35), institutions such as "the double granaries" (Strudwick, 1985: 264–71), and shifting and changing appointees representing the crown in the provinces (Martinet, 2011). Early in the Old Kingdom, small pyramids were placed at strategic points in the provincial landscape to emphasize royal power (Lehner, 1997: 96; Seidlmayer, 1996: 112). The state established a network of estates (Egyptian: *ḥwt*) throughout the delta and Nile Valley, the proceeds of which were owned and managed by the palace (Papazian, 2012: 37–39, 70–83; Moreno García, 1999). The produce of these helped support the building of large mortuary monuments as these required the crown to have access to large amounts of labor and resources.

At the same time, a large amount of economic activity existed on the provincial level outside of royal interest and investments – a "subsistence sphere" (Janssen 1979: 507–08; Eyre, 1999; Trigger, 1993: 11). Rather than treat these interests as peripheral to the state network (see Papazian, 2012: 30–31), I suggest we think of regional/local economic activities and identities as literally foundational to understanding integration of state and province.

The struggle in testing such a perspective is that data related to state identity and economy are present in the textual and monumental record and thus better preserved than evidence for smaller-scaled economic activities. Some provincial archaeological data do mitigate the disparity, pointing to local identities and local power. Provincial temples of the Old Kingdom existed with little connection to the king or central architectural styles, dedicated to local deities (Bussmann, 2014; Kemp, 2006: 116–35), suggesting localized spheres of activity. Art suggests the provincial elite played with centralized ideals and local ideologies, identities, and priorities (Vischak, 2015). That this independence and creativity should extend to some level of economic independence seems likely.

Ceramics can expand study of royal-private, royal-provincial economic integration, as all sites on this spectrum will yield pottery. The ubiquity of this artifact provides the opportunity to investigate Egyptian economic integration from the bottom up rather than the top down. Studying economic integration via the ceramic record includes working with vessel types that are known to have had economic value and are present at sites throughout Egypt. Additionally, the individual vessels must be dated by site-specific means. Strong site-specific dating can come from seriation or stratigraphy, rather than using the date from another, well-dated, parallel vessel coming from another site. Dating by parallel runs the risk of conflating regional difference and change (for example, comments in Hendrickx, 1996: 61).

Our example comes from the Old Kingdom beer jars (Egyptian: *ḏwiw*) and bread molds (Egyptian: *bḏꜣ* [*bedja*]; Figure 5). These vessels were used for the

Figure 5 Examples of Old Kingdom beer jar and *bedja* bread mold.
(photos by author)

preparation and distribution of bread and beer, commodities that formed the backbone of economic exchange and wage payment at the period by both royal and private individuals (Warden, 2014: 33–47). They were extraordinarily utilitarian, being hand built of the coarsest ceramic fabrics available to the potter and without surface finish or decoration. They are also the most common ceramics found at *any* Old Kingdom archaeological site. It is accordingly possible to examine a corpus of these types from Dynasties 1–6 and across the whole of the Egyptian state, thus investigating economic relationships across time and space.

As beer and bread were used for wage payments, the amount of each commodity an individual vessel held could have allowed for accounting (Bárta, 1996), as the vessel determined the amount of bread or beer both produced and distributed. Regulation of production or distribution of beer and bread would be visible in the volume of both beer jars and bread molds. Two hypotheses can be tested. A well-integrated, carefully controlled central economy would be evident in standardized beer and bread volumes. On the other hand, different standards for different sites would indicate regional control and smaller-scale integration; smaller-scale integration might indicate diverse authorities. Ultimately, both require that we test the standardization of many samples of beer jars and bread molds.

Standardization within an artifact assemblage may be measured using the Coefficient of Variation (CV) (Eerkens and Bettinger, 2001: 494–97). The CV is

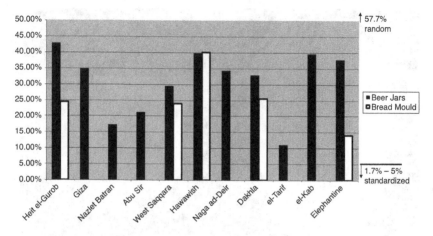

Figure 6 Simplified chart presenting CV distribution in Old Kingdom beer jars and bread mold samples from sites throughout Egypt. Samples are not fully contemporary. Within a site, the samples illustrated are each from a single dynasty. (chart by author)

a simple statistic: standard deviation/sample size * 100. It expresses the amount of variation of an attribute with a sample (Eerkens and Bettinger, 2001: 494–97). Ethnographic studies of ceramic manufacture show that potters producing standardized wares without external measuring devices create vessels with attributes having a CV of 5 percent (Eerkens, 2000; Longacre, 1999). Vessel standardization results from repeated muscle memory on the part of the potter. Within a CV of 5 percent or less variation exists but is minor, bounded by the limitations of human perception (Eerkens and Bettinger, 2001). The CVs for beer jar and bread mold volume were well above this threshold, meaning that volume was *not* standardized during the production. This held true at all sites under study, for all periods within the Old Kingdom and for all subtypes of beer jar and bread mold (Figure 6). The absence of standardization in the corpus means that beer and bread were not accounted for by a tightly centralized entity or even regional arms of such an institution (Warden, 2014: 81–168). Rather, the vessels represent a highly localized and personal system where a large number of potters manufactured the pots with no externally forced standard outside of the potters. Beer and bread production and exchange were local and individualized.

Even those vessel types with no clear economic role can yield implications of economic integration by signaling the scale of control over ceramic production. Large-scale standardization of types can only occur when a central authority

Figure 7 Meidum bowl attributes as measured by Sterling. (after Sterling, 2009: fig. 5. Redrawn by May Pwint Thair Chu and David S. Anderson, using KHPP G10.1-6-7.2)

controls production, enforcing a standard upon a manufacturing landscape encompassing many of the different potters across many a tremendous number of workshops. Standardization studies of Meidum bowls, the Old Kingdom fine ware bowl introduced in Section 2.2, shows that this vessel type exhibits degrees of variability. Variability fluctuates by attribute measured, such as diameter or angles of the rim (Figure 7) or the site from which the vessels came. Vessel diameter is the most regularized, with the lowest CV values in the study, while most other measurements show large amounts of variability (Sterling, 2009: tables 3–4; 2004, 196–202). These values show that the form was not standardized and, indeed, shows a level of localism. Yet that is only part of the picture.

Meidum bowls from Dynasty 4 (ca. 2575–2470 BC) assemblages from Giza and Elephantine show commonalities in their rim diameter and rim azimuth measurements. CVs of these attributes are similar. It follows that Dynasty 4 Meidum bowls from these two sites exhibited similar variation rim diameter and angles of the rim's recurve (Sterling, 2004: 213). The mean values of these measurements are further confirmed to be similar through Analysis of Variance (ANOVA) and Discriminant Function Comparisons (Sterling, 2015: 57–63). Such a strong similarity suggests increased contact between the two areas, probably the result of Elephantine supplying granite for major royal building projects. Perhaps potters themselves moved between sites as part of the building process (Sterling, 2004: 154, 208–13, 225–26, 228). Meidum bowls from sites less involved in state activities, such as Kom el-Hisn in the western Delta, show locally scaled, independent variation. State building projects provided a point of integration into the provinces, influencing the ceramic industry, echoing the evidence of CD7 discussed in Section 2.2. Yet Sterling's finding is more nuanced, highlighting that integration was not overarching but rather existed at multiple scales of interaction, dependent in part upon local environment, the settlement's agricultural sustainability, and the needs of monument building (Sterling, 2015: 63–64; 2004: 228–31).

Consistent in the above studies are findings that the state did not exert economic dominance in daily life or exchange. Royal economic networks might have been quite removed from provincial settlements and local life. The evidence suggests that private individuals had control over their own wealth. The variability in vessel volumes further argues for a barter economy where value was personally negotiated through face-to-face relationships (Warden, 2014: 249–53) and relationships that might have been further determined by patronage ties, for which there is growing evidence (Campagno, 2014; Warden, 2014; Moreno García, 2013; Eyre, 2011). Ceramic analyses emphasize that provincial individuals experienced a complex economic life existing on several scales: local, small-scale barter relationships and occasional state influences, at minimum. Local activities formed networks that did not exist as peripherals to the royal economic network. It is possible that for an average ancient Egyptian the royal network existed peripherally to their own economic activities, especially as the Old Kingdom state was not yet expansive enough to tax individuals (Warden, 2015). Egyptian economy in the third millennium BC did not act as two spheres (royal versus provincial). Rather, there were many local spheres that interacted with, but do not appear to have been well-integrated with, the royal administration (see also Bussmann, 2014).

2.5 Conclusion

This section demonstrated how, by collecting detailed data on the attributes of common ceramic types, the ceramic record shows Old Kingdom Egypt to have been culturally integrated but not defined by the royal house – the opposite, in many ways, of how modern history books present Egyptian society. State economy existed beside and outside local and private economic activity. Meanwhile, obvious socioeconomic differences marked by larger tombs and access to high quality materials for the elite were mitigated in part through access to and use of the same ceramics by all Egyptians, perhaps even access to the same potters. These ceramics were used in similar ways across classes, marking common activities across the social spectrum. One must expect that economic and cultural integration fluctuated and changed over time, being redefined and reestablished as Egyptian royal power expanded over the millennia. The ceramic records of later periods, such as (but not limited to) the Middle and New Kingdoms, can be explored using similar methods. The lesser-known corpora of the First and Second Intermediate Periods have the potential to also show local identities and power – especially valuable when compared to data from the unified periods that flank them.

3 Investigating Egyptian Regionalism

Study of the Egyptian state conjures a picture of unity, a territory held under one government. Accordingly, study of the state necessitates that data reflecting the pharaoh and his bureaucracy are central to the discourse. If we turn to studying Egyptian culture and thinking about the Egyptian Nile Valley through a more anthropological lens, unity is no longer a given and the royal house decentered. Egyptian culture – like any culture – was dynamic (for overview, see Schneider, 2003: 155–57). As we have seen, the state did not necessarily dictate religion, economy, social interaction, the arts, or any of the myriad of institutions which make up cultural identity. The establishment of a state does not preclude the presence of regional identities, as most readers can attest from their lived experiences.

It seems certain that regionalism existed in ancient Egypt. The environment fostered it. Egypt's water regime was localized. Egyptians were reliant upon natural basins present in the landscape to take advantage of the Nile flood; these basins enforced a type of agriculture that encouraged local cooperation but did not require large-scale integration (Lehner, 2000; Butzer, 1976). The movement of the Nile over millennia was not experienced equally across the country but rather varied regionally, forcing populations to be locally responsive to their changing environment (Schneider and Johnston, 2020; Bunbury et al., 2017; Hillier et al., 2007). Local landscapes in turn supported local identities, some of which are evident in the artistic record (Vischak, 2015). The extent to which the Nile's regionalism affected material culture can be tested using the abundant and ever-present ceramic evidence. This section will present some of the ways that the ceramic record corroborates and expands our understanding of regionalism in the Egyptian cultural landscape.

3.1 Theories and Methods

Note that throughout this section both *regional* and *local* are used, sometimes interchangeably, to express substate units. I will nominally treat *regional* as referring to a larger physical area than *local*. As the data do not often allow for fine, city-scale, resolution, I will more often use *regional*.

Identifying regionalism in the ceramic record can be done by turning to ceramic production, identifying regional or local clays, forms, and variations within ceramic types. Unfortunately, very few ceramic workshops of this period are known (e.g., Verner, 1993; Soukiassian et al., 1990; Kaiser et al., 1982), so one must collect production data from the sherds and vessels themselves. The stronger the regional markers are in the ceramic record, the more diverse the industry. The more diverse the industry, the more numerous and diverse the authorities controlling it. By extension, regional ceramic production opens the door to regional agency, whether corporate or individual, and regional or even local identities. Regionalism in pottery, then, speaks not just to ceramic production but also to variations in cultural identity.

This discussion has roots in Craft Production Theory, which aims to determine mode of production and its relationship to social and political systems (e.g., Roux, 2019: 284; Köhler, 2008; Sinopoli, 2003: 13–37; Costin, 2001; Rice, 1987: 181–84). Much of Craft Production Theory is concerned with the question of whether potters were specialists, trained and dedicated to making pottery, or nonspecialists, producing only for their own needs. For specialist production, the additional question is how labor was controlled. Some of these data were presented in Section 2.2, where we noted that Egyptian potters during the period in question seem to have been specialists trained and dedicated to making pottery at least part, if not all, of the year, at the supra-household level (Warden, 2014: 174–89; 2011; Köhler, 1997). Understanding who controlled these specialists, however, requires that we turn to identify the presence or absence of regionalization in the record.

Investigating the ceramic *chaînes opératoires* can further help us understand how production is managed and influences society, from the initial point of clay acquisition to the terminus of distribution of completed vessels (Roux, 2019: 283–316). *Chaînes opératoires* studies focus not simply on the technical chain of production but on the activities related to each technical stage. Thus, technology becomes an indicator of social activity and social structuring. Here we will focus only on the beginning and end of ceramic production – clay acquisition and vessel distribution. The former has the potential to show location of production, the latter the exchange relationships between regions. Both can be investigated by looking at a pot's fabric, through both visual examination to archaeometric techniques such as petrography and Neutron Activation Analysis (NAA).

Any archaeological theory requires careful data acquisition, as the possibility of identifying regional chains is lost if data are aggregated or synthesized too early. The ceramicist should bear this in mind when recording raw data, keeping site-specific notes, typologies, and sequences over the length of the work at a site. Once the site-specific framework is built (on paper, in the database, and in physical sherd libraries when possible) one may put the material into discussion with that from other sites without losing any local identifiers. Finding regionalism in the record requires identifying diversity – something that cannot be done if one imposes a standardized framework on the material from the outset.

3.2 Ceramic Production

The material that constitutes a pottery vessel is called the vessel's fabric. Fabric bears a relationship to the plastic clay paste from which it was made, though with chemical and compositional changes due to firing (Nordström, 2011: 724–25; Bourriau et al., 2000: 129). The landmark volume for Egyptian ceramic studies, *An Introduction to Ancient Egyptian Pottery* (Arnold and Bourriau, 1993), presented a codification of Egyptian fabrics called "The Vienna System" (Nordström and Bourriau, 1993). The result of collaboration between archaeologists working on sites throughout Egypt, the Vienna System was designed to be flexible, presenting broad fabric types identified from Egyptian ceramic samples from the Middle Kingdom through the middle of the New Kingdom (ca. 2000–1300 BC). The main distinction, Nile versus marl clay, divides clays mined from Nile alluvium from those calcareous (limestone-based) clays mined from the desert and its margins.[2] It does not include Oasis or Aswan fabrics which were and are regionally distinct.

The basic Nile/marl division provides a peek into regional production of Egyptian ceramics. Settlements throughout Egypt had easy access to Nile clays while marls were more regionally distinct, being fully dependent upon local geology. Potters who manufactured Nile clay vessels could be based at almost any settlement and need not have gone long distances to access raw material. Those potters working with marls were themselves likely based close to the marl clay's source. Marl vessels could not be ubiquitously produced throughout Egypt because the material itself was not available everywhere; thus, attaining a marl vessel was more likely to require a trade network between settlements. Further subdivision within these Nile and marl categories is based on type and amount of inclusions observed in the cross section (Figure 8). The Vienna System provided scholars a uniform language and systematic approach for reference and analysis of Egyptian ceramic fabrics. For the purposes of this Element, it is particularly key as it is the dominant fabric typology applied to Old through Middle Kingdom sherds.

The Vienna System allows ceramicists and archaeologists to compare material across sites (see also Bourriau, 2007). Such comparison is crucial if we are to understand how Egyptian culture, as well as the Egyptian state, related and interacted across space. However, uncritical, "plug and play" application of the Vienna System can cause ceramicists to manufacture unity and standardization.

---

[2] Nile clays have often been referred to as "Nile silts" or "Nile silt clays." However, "silt" and "clay" refer to different sediment sizes, with clay being finer than silt. Using these two terms together confuses the definition and the term should be updated to "Nile clay" (Ownby, personal communication).

Figure 8 Examples of Nile versus Marl clay as visible in cross section under simple (in this case, photographic) magnification. (photos by author)

Any typology has an element of the subjective, and textual descriptions are individually interpreted and differentially translated from published text to physical sherd. The same fabric of the Vienna System can be seen and applied differently by different analysts while still providing a veneer of objectivity (Raue, 2018b: 198). Overapplication of the Vienna fabrics can also allow one to make poor assumptions of applicability and unity in ceramic production, thus conflating data from multiple sites.

The best balance as currently carried out in the field is for ceramicists to establish local fabric typologies that can then be paralleled, when possible, to fabrics in the Vienna System. Creating a local fabric series requires the ceramicist to look specifically at their sample, open up to the possibilities of difference, and acknowledge what they can identify as an individual analyst. The local system allows for identification of local trends in production, while parallels to the Vienna System enable broader discussions of cross-site materials. Once a system exists for a site, it should continue to be used rather than created anew out of whole cloth.

Determining fabric requires that the ceramicist views a fresh break, made parallel to the rim, under magnification. It is typically easiest to work with a hand lens (10× magnification) for field analysis, but best to work with a binocular microscope (20–30× magnification) for initial definition and description of fabric groups (Nordström, 2011: 726). For each sherd, the ceramicist notes fabric density and hardness, coloration at the break, and inclusions (type, size, frequency). Similar sherds will be grouped together as identifiable, consistent characteristics begin to emerge; such groups become the basis of each fabric group. Field fabric series based on visual identification can be tested through lab analyses. The level of specificity such lab analyses yield is difficult to reproduce in fieldwork and tends to answer different research questions, so likely will serve separate research purposes (e.g., Ownby, 2016, 2009; Rzeuska and Ownby, 2009). A local fabric series, complete with detailed text, photos of fresh breaks, and parallels to the Vienna System, must be published if it is to be any use for synthetic analyses or future work. It is also best to store labeled samples of each fabric type on-site for training and to ensure the long-term viability of a system for future researchers at a site.

Differences in fabrics can be used to illustrate the local scale of Egyptian ceramic production. To illustrate this, let us begin with the primary groups of fabrics used in Egyptian pottery: Nile and marl clays.

The matrix for Nile clays is visually similar throughout the Nile Valley, leaving the identification of inclusions as the primary way to differentiate Nile clay fabrics. Study of inclusions has revealed locally specific variation in otherwise similar fabrics. For example, Nile clay sherds at Tell el-Dab'a typically include "scattered rounded sand grains," even in fabrics otherwise parallel to the Vienna System. Such grains are generally absent from Nile clay sherds found at Upper Egyptian sites. The rounded sand grains seem to derive from the geology of the Nile Delta, thus marking Tell el-Dab'a's Nile clay pottery production as originating in the delta (Aston, 2004: 32; Ownby, personal communication). Inclusions can also reveal site- and period-specific fabrics. Fabric NEL1 at Elephantine, used from the Fifth through the mid-Sixth Dynasties, can be identified through its lack of inclusions, fine preparation, and colorful phasing at the break (Raue, 2018b: 198). Rare Fabric I-b-3, found at Tell el-Dab'a during the late Second Intermediate Period, is defined by its inclusion of mica and quartz particles that can be up to 1 mm in size, as well as an ash-gray central zone at the break (Aston, 2004: 32). Such fabrics indicate that local developments in ceramic production and distribution were not just influenced by the local environment, but were also local choices manifest at specific moments in time.

Inclusions do not provide the only key to fabric identification. Sometimes, the archaeologist might find sherds that "feel different" from the rest of the corpus. The difference might be marked by surface treatment or texture. It could perhaps just be a gut feeling that arises in the analyst from being immersed in the material. For example, Saqqara Fabric P.60 was identified first due to the distinctive surface and texture of sherds of this material and then confirmed through petrographic analysis (Rzeuska and Ownby, 2009; Rzeuska, 2006: 42). It is a mixture of Nile clay and marl clays only known in Saqqara during the Old Kingdom (Rzeuska, 2006: 42–44; though similar also at Memphis, Ownby personal communication). Sherds of this fabric exhibit variable range and amount of inclusions, both organic and inorganic. Identifying local production may require careful, detailed knowledge of the corpus at hand.

Local fabric series established by visual analysis in the field often emphasize the potter's choices in production by focusing on inclusions and seeking to identify paste preparation. Lab analyses, on the other hand, are more able to approach geological realities. NAA allows analysts to identify elements present in a fabric sample, further substantiating the argument that Nile clay pottery was produced locally. NAA has shown Nile clay sherds from Tell el-Dab'a and Dahshur to have distinctive chemical signatures, identified as due to geological differences in local clays. The same seems to be true of Nile clay vessels from Memphis and Askut (Bourriau et al., 2006: 268, 270).

NAA will be hard if not impossible for most analysts to apply to their material. Petrography, on the other hand, may be done on-site. This archaeometric analysis allows for investigation of clay origins and methods of production through analysis of a thin section of the ceramic under a polarizing light microscope (Braekmans and Degryse, 2016: 234). It could be fruitfully brought to bear on these questions, though it is underutilized for Nile clay sherds. Petrography has illuminated differences between New Kingdom Nile clays from Memphis and Tell el-Amarna (Bourriau et al., 2000). The differences identified via NAA and petrographic analyses derive from local geological differences, allowing for discussion of production and distribution of a vessel.

Nile clay pottery suggests that much of ceramic production was probably local, using local materials. Large-scale movement of Nile clay vessels does not seem to have occurred. Marl clays complicate the picture by providing evidence for ceramic production and trade across regions. NAA analysis shows marl clay samples form tight chemical groups, indicating that each marl comes from a different region; each type of marl pottery analyzed was made in one place and distributed outwards (Bourriau et al., 2006: 273–77). Indications that marl clays were mined and produced in specific regions might seem to negate the need for creating a local typology of marl clays (and indeed, the marls referenced here are largely identified via the Vienna System), but marl production could potentially derive from many different points of origin. Indeed, the precision and care used in creating a local system can allow the ceramicist to identify new regional marls (such as Marl F; see Aston, 2004: 35) or potential mixes of marl and Nile clays that might then be further tested (Ownby, 2016: 466–67; Rzeuska and Ownby, 2009).

Unfortunately, marls' chemical groupings cannot be tied to the clays' geographic origin as we lack knowledge of the chemical compositions of Egyptian clays (Ownby, 2016: 462; 2011: 756; Bourriau et al., 2006: 273–76). Instead, identifying marl clay sources has been done via fall-off analysis: the careful quantification of frequency of marl sherds and diversity of marl vessel types found at different sites. The higher the percentage of a specific marl in a ceramic corpus and the greater the variety of vessel types made in that marl clay, the more likely the source of the clay is nearby. Sites with fewer sherds and vessel types of a given marl would have probably received the vessels through trade with a distant point of manufacture, with fewer marl vessels of more limited forms appearing as one moves further from the source. Thus, the best way to identify the region of marl production is to be able to compare sherd quantification and typology across sites. Such work suggests that Marl C is Memphite in origin (Bader, 2002: 31, 53; 2001); Marl A, Upper Egyptian (Rzeuska, 2011: 493); and Marl B from the region around Ballas, again in Upper Egypt (Bourriau, 1990). Comparison of marl ceramic corpora provides evidence for regional difference and cross-regional interaction as vessels were exchanged.[3] The comparative method used for determining marl origin would be useful to apply to discussion of any fabric in order to understand regional differences. However, it is difficult to do because raw numbers (sherd weights, counts, percentages by locus or period) are rarely published.

Moving forward, there is great potential for the integration of archaeometric techniques in ceramic study. Lab techniques can be difficult to integrate into Egyptian field projects due to restriction on exporting archaeological material and the constantly changing face of technology. However, petrography is promising especially as it can be conducted on-site; X-ray Florescence Spectrometry (XRF/pXRF) could also aid compositional analysis without any real lab needs (Holmqvist, 2016; Ownby, 2011: 763; Ownby, 2009). It is important to remember that archaeometry can come to different results and, like all archaeological analyses, it is best to combine conventional and lab techniques. There is no magic wand, only more data.

3.3 Assessing Localism and Regionalism via Typologies

Though the majority of vessels were locally produced of Nile clays and not widely distributed from their place of production, their relationship to local culture, and if there is one, remains to be proven. Detailed formal analysis of vessel typologies reveals variation site-to-site that can help elucidate the links between local production and local identity. Variation at the site level can be the result of a host of factors, including production for different venues such as settlement or cemetery (Bourriau, 1986–87); different local tastes, activities,

---

[3] When trading, the Egyptians were not seeking to exchange vessels. Rather, the goods within the vessels were traded, and likely the container itself was incidental. Archaeological preservation encourages us to focus on something that, to the Egyptians, was probably a secondary concern.

and associated demands; and even variation between individual potters (for example, Gandon et al., 2020).

The types discussed here are largely identified by archaeologists and not by the ancient Egyptians. These "devised types" are based on formal attributes such as morphology and size (Rice, 1987: 275–77). Fabric may also be used as one of a type's defining attributes. Though devised typologies do not necessarily accord with the ancient typologies ("folk typology": Rice, 1987: 277–82) studies relating the art historic and ceramic records help draw a relationship between the two (Faltings, 1998). Each project should maintain its own devised typology of the ceramics they have identified at the site, to be expanded as necessary. Comparing ceramic typologies from different sites and employing them to understand the presence or absence of ceramic types at a site provides evidence useful for discussion of local function and identity.

Producing a typology requires both knowledge of Egyptian ceramic corpora writ large and careful visual examination of material from a given site. The ceramic corpus of Egyptian sites during Kingdoms is *recognizable* across Egypt; that does not mean all vessels are the same. Yet there is no need to redefine well-known types, for example the Old Kingdom Meidum bowl already discussed. For the Old and Middle Kingdoms, useful typologies can be found in reports (for example, Reisner and Smith, 1955) and ceramic compendia (for example, Schiestl and Seiler, 2012a). A project-specific typ-ology should seek to employ the familiar types found in these sources, deter-mine if there is any local variation within these types and identify any novel types. Dietrich Raue's work at Elephantine provides a good example (Raue, 2018b). He established local ceramic phases at the site, determining chrono-logical blocks in which different vessel types were produced. Using this phas-ing, he further created a local typology of Meidum bowls, identifying chronological change in the form that is both locally specific and finer grained than any other dating system for Meidum bowls (Figure 9; see also Beeck, 2004).

Types may be defined based upon a hierarchy of attributes. Typically, one separates "open" from "closed" forms, this loosely being the difference between bowls (open forms) and jars (closed forms). Other attributes, such as vessel morphology and size, rim morphology and diameter, or vessel fabric also merit consideration and will be ranked differently depending on the preservation of the sample. For instance, if a sample has many complete vessels, it is good policy to let vessel shape be a relatively high-ranking attribute in the typology. Complete vessels, after all, yield the most data. However, in settlement excava-tions complete vessels are notable in their absence and thus rim morphology and size must be our guiding attributes (see Bader, 2016, 2010 for challenges).

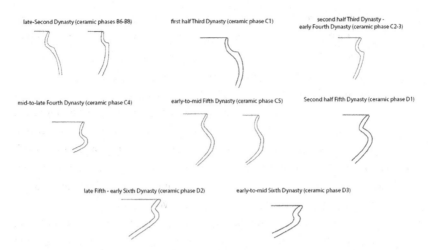

Figure 9 Meidum Bowl typology for Elephantine Island (drawn by author after Raue, 2018b: Abb. 78.10, .11; 79.1, .4, .8, .11; 80.1, .9, .11). Note this demonstrates when new forms were introduced and not how long a given form was manufactured.

Typology creation is necessarily influenced by the analyst as typologies will always present vague or ambiguous cases and the individual archaeologist will have to make many judgment calls (Adams and Adams, 1991). Seeing more sherds and vessels in both real life and in publication is necessary for making a good typology. Typologies should be published whenever possible and include quantification (diameter ranges, percentages preserved, frequency in the corpus). Once armed with a site-specific typology, one can compare it to typologies from other sites, identifying formal variation across space and time and types unique to a specific site. Comparing individual site typologies is fundamental in identifying regionalism in the archaeological record.

Local production of pottery does not mean that potters were uninfluenced by objects and people they encountered through cross-site contact. Both localism and regionalism existed in ancient Egypt; interaction and identity were multi-scalar. Typological studies provide evidence that, despite pottery's tendency for local production, types were affected by interactions within subregions of Egypt as early as the Predynastic Period (Köhler, 2014b). A classic example comes from Stephen Seidlmayer's (1990) study of First Intermediate Period pottery (ca. 2160–2050). The First Intermediate Period was an era of weakened government authority sandwiched by the centralized power of the Old and Middle Kingdoms. During this period, Seidlmayer shows that two broad typological divisions arise. Jar types became elongated and thin in Lower Egypt while they became bag-shaped in Upper Egypt (Seidlmayer, 1990). The straightforward divide into two regions might obscure developments within smaller subregions. Very specific paralleling of First Intermediate Period vessels from the Fayum-area cemetery of Sedment reveals a "more or less independent and unparalleled development of ceramic material" in the Memphis-Fayyum region (Bader, 2012: 233).

The regional differences between jars points to a breaking of the cultural network during the First Intermediate Period. Lower Egyptian sites interacted more with each other than with Upper Egyptian sites and vice versa, with perhaps more intense interaction occurring between smaller subregions as Bader's work suggests. Such restricted contact is not just a sign of government fracturing but also highlights a shrinkage of spheres of cultural interaction and the appearance, or perhaps simply a new visual manifestation, of two Egyptian identities in a way not known since the middle of the Naqada Period (ca. 3200 BC). It remains to test the Old and Middle Kingdom corpus in a similar way to explore the scale of cultural unification during periods of royal strength (see Section 3.4).

Typology can also highlight local difference and specialization. For example, upon occasion a ceramic type is present at only one site – this is a presence/ absence study. Such cases can indicate a special function of a vessel type and, by extension, of the site. Alternately, unique ceramic types might illustrate local styles or trends. One example is the flat-based rough ware beaker (Type 38) known at South Abydos during the late Middle Kingdom (Figure 10; Wegner, 2007: 242). Abundant numbers of rough ware beakers were found around the doorways of the mortuary temple of Senwosret III, where they seem to have been regularly discarded after use in the temple (Wegner et al., 2000: 104, 106–07). The deposition of these vessels marks them as a basic tool in the royal cult of the late Middle Kingdom. It is impossible to know if this was common practice during the late Middle Kingdom; no other Middle Kingdom mortuary temples have been excavated in modern times. However, early Middle Kingdom mortuary temples are missing the rough ware beaker type and instead use an abundance of miniature vessels (see Arnold, 1988a), suggesting, at the least, diachronic change in royal cultic practice. It is possible, though not certain, that these beakers were specific to the cult of Senwosret III at Abydos.

3.4 Egyptian and Foreign

Presence/absence studies of ceramics often yield "foreign" sherds and vessels, markers of cross-cultural interactions throughout Egypt that varied in type and scale by site. We must be careful not to treat pots as people and it is not clear who made or owned these foreign vessels. Foreign vessels (manufactured elsewhere) and foreign-style vessels (of non-Egyptian type, manufactured locally) typically appear in small numbers at Egyptian settlements and have poor statistical value.

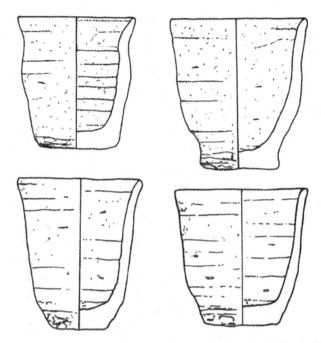

Figure 10 Late Middle Kingdom rough ware beaker from South Abydos.
(Wegner, 2007: fig. 125.96-99; used with permission
of Josef Wegner)

Their meaning, however, far outstrips their number. Their simple presence – often of locally produced clays – complicates ideas of Egyptian identity, suggesting that different towns had different levels of knowledge of and interaction with ideas, objects, and perhaps people from other cultures.

Ceramics show cultural mixing at several settlement sites. The scale of the foreign corpus is notable at Elephantine during the Predynastic-Middle Kingdoms and Tell el-Dab'a of the late Middle Kingdom and Second Intermediate Period. At Elephantine, the regular appearance of Nubian sherds in most archaeological contexts, though in small numbers after the Early Dynastic Period, has been interpreted as meaning Nubians and Egyptians both lived on the island. Through constant contact they created a joint assemblage resulting from locally specific cultural evolution (Raue, 2008; see also Raue, 2002). Levantine-style pottery, both imported from the Levant and produced locally, is present at the town of Tell el-Dab'a (Bader, 2010: 211; Aston, 2004: 102–55). These vessels appear to indicate a local subculture arising in the eastern Delta, mixing both Egyptian and Levantine traits. Cultural mixing might be anticipated at Elephantine and Tell el-Dab'a, as their locations – Elephantine on the First Cataract and bordering Nubia, Tell el-Dab'a in the eastern Delta and close to the Levant – mark them clearly as borders. Yet most sites in the Nile Valley can be considered in some ways to be borders, as they edge the desert, a fuzzy boundary full of chaos, nomads, and foreigners. The deserts created a porous border that would have allowed for cross-cultural interaction that could affect local culture and interactions at almost all Egyptian sites.

No region should be automatically assumed to have been isolated from relationships with foreign individuals – or, at least, foreign goods. The occasional Nubian sherd has even been found in the delta settlement of Kom el-Hisn (Kirby et al., 1998: 30, 39). Imported Levantine vessels are known in Old Kingdom Egyptian tombs through the Old Kingdom, with the majority coming from Dynasty 4 elite tombs in the Memphite necropolis. Occasional finds in provincial tombs of the mid-late Old Kingdom suggest that even nonroyal Egyptians were aware of the foreign world to the north and either interacted with it in direct trade relationships or through down-the-line trade (Sowada, 2009: 54–90, 180–82; see Section 5 for further discussion). Thus, foreign ceramics highlight different scales of interaction and access to goods across Egypt.

3.5 Multi-Scalar Interaction

As already noted, unlike the First Intermediate Period, the Old and Middle Kingdom pottery corpora look similar across Egypt. It is tempting to equate similarity with sameness or standardization and, by extension, one monolithic culture. However, studies of the variation within a single vessel type of attributes such as rim shape, diameter measurements, or vessel height have shown that seemingly standardized types do vary across sites. Such studies require access to large numbers of vessels, often from multiple sites, to build robust, statistically significant samples. Data may be collected through fieldwork or literature review, though ceramic publications do not always present quantification of their material. It can be difficult to assemble a dataset and accordingly such studies are in their infancy in Egyptian archaeology.

Some vessel attributes easily lend themselves to measurement and numeric summation: diameter and height, for instance. Others, such as the shape of a vessel's rim, may be accounted for by measuring segment lengths and angles of rim. This complex approach is modeled by Sarah Sterling's (2009, 2004) study of Meidum bowls, a common Old Kingdom fine ware. Sterling measured multiple attributes at the rim of each vessel and then compared Meidum bowl samples across sites: Elephantine, Qau/Badari, Meidum, Heit el-Ghurob, and Kom el-Hisn (Figure 7). The consistency of these values, and by extension the consistency of rim shape, across sites was then tested using ANOVA. ANOVA tests the likelihood that variability between mean values from assemblages at different sites resulted from chance, allowing one to identify true variability between sites (McCall, 2018: 80–86). When ANOVA tests are applied to the measurements from all the sites, as controlled for chronology, Sterling's results show both that there is variation in Meidum bowl rim morphology between sites and that variation is the result of true differences in vessel morphology at different sites. In brief, Meidum bowl shape varied by locality (Sterling, 2009: 171-182). These findings help explain why typological studies of the Meidum bowl that have grouped material from across Egypt together have found great variation in some variables unrelated to simple chronological evolution (Beeck, 2004: 260–61, 265–68) and why local typologies, such as Raue's above, are most effective.

Measurement need not always be so complex to document a vessel type's change over time or space. Diameter and vessel height are easy to measure in the field and can be expressed as a relationship called a *vessel index*: (maximum diameter/height) × 100. This relationship was used by Dorothea Arnold (1988b: 140–41) at Lisht to develop a seriation of hemispherical cups, a common Middle Kingdom vessel type (Figure 11). Her work shows that the relationship of rim diameter to height in hemispherical cups has chronological relevance, with older cups being wider and squatter, only to become deeper and narrower over time. Her seriation has been applied to sites throughout Egypt and often found to be a good fit for development of the form elsewhere (for example: Kopp, 2019; Bagh, 2012). However, the values do not always fit: Tell el-Dab'a is an outlier, where the shape of the vessels underwent specifically local development that is not in keeping with what is seen at other Lower Egyptian sites (Bagh, 2012: 31–32). Thus, vessel index, when applied to hemispherical cups, shows both national and local trends, implying multiscale interaction.

Additional quantification is necessary to further such studies and allow for statistical analysis. If done *in tandem* with seriation, these values would help us understand the full scale of variability of production (or lack thereof) within and across sites. Numbers, of course, present only one part of the picture. In the case of hemispherical cups, numbers hide local variation in other vessel attributes: for example, while Elephantine's hemispherical cups seem to follow larger trends in vessel index, they do not show the same patterning in surface treatment found in Lisht and Dahshur and rather exhibit local variation (Kopp, 2019).

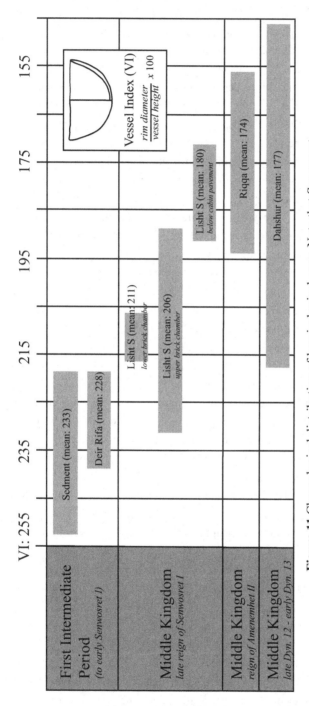

Figure 11 Chronological distribution of hemispherical cups. Note that Senwosret I and Amenemhet II are the first two kings of Dynasty 12. (drawn by author after Arnold, 1988b: 140–46, fig. 75)

Analysis of vessel attributes presents a complex picture of diverse interaction and the scale of production.

3.6 Conclusion

The production and distribution of ceramics encourages us to think of Egyptian identity as multi-scalar, with local/regional variability. The bulk of ceramic production was local, dominated by Nile clay wares. It might be tempting to see in this trend a nationally-scaled choice, but it was more likely just potters' pragmatic response to what materials were easiest to access. Local ceramic production in Nile clays can show local, diachronic change (e.g., Elephantine Fabric NEL 1, Tell el-Dab'a Fabric I-b-3) as well as local innovation in paste preparation (e.g., Saqqara Fabric P.60). Ceramic production occasionally even yielded forms specific to a site or a site's function (e.g., the South Abydos beaker). Marl clays, on the other hand, highlight that the ceramic industry could be tied to geologically specific places, promoting exchange within and across regions. As marl clay vessels are the minority of most corpora, trade across regions currently appears to have been limited, leaving localities to mostly local production and goods. Production of pottery, and presumably the goods it contained, was seemingly a place of local control and autonomy.

This is not to lose sight of the fact that the ceramic record shows that interaction and identity were multi-scalar, influenced by exchange of ideas and interactions between people. Meidum bowls show both local variability by site and, as illustrated in Section 2, influence between sites related to royal building projects. Typological variability is regionalized in the First Intermediate Period. The differential presence of foreign ceramic wares further emphasizes that Egyptians across Egypt were not uniform communities with homogenous access to standard goods. Instead, variability marked the material landscape, a diversity in things that indicates localisms within lived practice, experiences, and identity across the Nile Valley.

4 The Relationship of Political to Social Change

Egyptian historical chronology as it stands is a political chronology, a series of Kingdoms and Intermediate Periods, terms created by modern scholars and tied to the fortunes of the kingship. This chronology has been refined periodically and assigned absolute (numerical/calendrical) dates, often through ^{14}C dating. However, ^{14}C delivers the wide range of dates. In practice, much of Egyptian dating is a relative chronology where temporal order is apparent but specific years unclear. Thus, dating Egyptian archaeological materials generally relies on the relative framework of dynasties and kings' names, rather than absolute numerical dates (see Dee, 2017; Shortland and Ramsey, 2013; Dee et al., 2008; Hendrickx, 2006: 90).

Most excavation directors will want, and need, the ceramicist to use the historical chronology in dating the ceramic material. Ceramics are often used to provide dates for any finds in the same context (the assemblage) and the surrounding deposit (the locus or strata). Ceramics essentially provide a date for all cultural activity at the site. As a result, the ceramicist will often be asked to know the dynasty during which the sherd was produced and/or used: better, a phase within that dynasty (i.e., early/mid/late), more rarely a specific reign (e.g., Senwosret I).   .

In this way, ceramics are used to support and apply Egyptian chronology to the archaeological record. The tension is that cultural change does not occur in direct relationship to political change. Change as encapsulated in the historic record – the death of one king and the installation of another, or the rise of a new dynasty – are abrupt moments that do not correspond to large-scale cultural changes. People generally continued eating the same foods, using the same cooking installations, trading the same commodities, and practicing the same rituals throughout moments of political upheaval.

Material culture is the material of cultural practice, physical objects that enable and enact those things we as people do, from cooking to ritual acts to trade and everything in between. Change in material culture provides a window into how cultural activities and interactions might have transformed over time. Numerous cultural variables affect ceramics types and styles and result in change: technology (such as the introduction of the wheel), social relationships (with other cities or cultures), religious significance (such as ceramic use in funerary rituals), food production (preparation of ingredients and recipes), economic relationships (via the distribution of goods), as well as cultural mores and tastes (see also Rice, 1987: 245–46). These are all sociocultural variables and *not* political variables. As a result, the same vessel types carry over from one historic moment to the next.

Historical change affects daily life to some extent, but at a distance and a delay that minimizes its chronological relationship to cultural change. When a king died, no ceramic types were automatically retired or introduced (Figure 12). Quick, widespread adoption of a ceramic type is the exception, rather than the rule, of typological change. Sudden introduction of new ceramic types can occur and is often related to sudden changes in ritual, particularly court-level ritual (Section 2.3; see also Seiler, 2005: 161–84; specific examples Bárta, 1995a: 16). More typically, since pottery was an easily produced, low-status good, it reflects political, elite change less clearly than prestige goods (Rice, 1987: 456–68).

"THANK GOODNESS NEXT WEEK WE'LL BE IN
A NEW DYNASTY AND WE CAN MAKE SOME
OTHER STYLE OF POTTERY."

Figure 12 *Not* how Egyptian pottery production worked. (copyright Theresa
McCracken; reprinted with artist's permission)

Ceramics provide variable levels of evidence for chronological change.
Different types change at different paces; some do not seem to change at all.
Stylistic change is commonly accepted as occurring more quickly in well-made
table wares as they were for public-facing use. Functional, utilitarian forms, on
the other hand, sometimes show less change as they play fundamental roles in
food processing and storage, practices that change very slowly.[4] Such vessels
were not widely displayed. The slow change of utilitarian wares sits in direct
opposition to their frequent breakage and discard, as documented ethnograph-
ically (Skibo, 2013: 3; Longacre, 1985). For a vessel to be a good chronological
indicator, it must be a common type that shows frequent change. The bulk of the
ceramic record does not fit this category, so if one is interested in is dating, one
will of necessity ignore most of the corpus.

---

[4] Though this is not always the case: for the Old Kingdom beer jar see Rzeuska (2006: 380–88).

Political chronology and ceramic chronology each result from different processes and express different relationships. In pharaonic Egypt, the absence of central control over ceramic production means that ceramic change results from changing social mores and relationships, a shifting that is the result of multivariate pressures occurring at a regional or local level, more parallel than top down. The further away from the center a potter operated, the less likely his workshop was related to the royal house. The pace of change for archaeological ceramics is thus more complex, often slower and less abrupt than political change. Accordingly, site reports often present a site-specific ceramic phasing that is equated to political periods but that are not in one-to-one concordance with dynastic dates (e.g., Raue, 2018b: 188–97; Bourriau and Gallorini, 2016: 212; Rzeuska, 2006: 383). Regardless, it is fundamentally important to also translate a ceramic phase date into a phase in the historic chronology. Only by giving a political date can archaeological work be tied into and affect a national-level historic narrative.

At the same time, we must be aware that by making a ceramic date into a historic, and therefore political, date what we are engaging in is fundamentally an act of translation. Political and ceramic chronologies do not denote the same expanses of time. When we employ ceramics only to translate their information into political chronology, the ceramic record's relationship to the pace and narrative of cultural change is subsumed by the narrative of political history. The chronology constrains us. Ceramics provide a counter narrative, illuminating both social change and consistency, both of which occur out of sync with changes in the royal house. Ceramics, then, can be used to trace change over time in social practices (such as food production) and larger systems (such as economic systems), helping us uncover a social history of ancient Egypt.

This section will not spend much time working through the fundamentals of dating pottery. Other texts will help the reader gain more information of dating methodologies (Orton and Hughes, 2013: 219–34; Rice, 1987: 435–43), and some information is provided in the Glossary. Instead, this section will introduce the social implications of ceramic change (or: dates) and how ceramic chronology encourages us to think about continuity and evolution of Egyptian culture from its grassroots.

4.1 Theories and Methods

Cultural change is not monolithic but rather occurs differentially in different spheres of activity. Ceramic types thus would have changed at different paces depending on their function and social role. Tracing diachronic change within ceramic types can be done by tracing shifts in a vessel's style. "Style" is a term colloquially easy to apply but archaeologically difficult to quantify (see, for example, exhaustive discussions in Conkey and Hastorf, 1990; Rice, 1987: 244–73). At its most basic, style is a way in which something is made, resulting from human choice among a series of options (Hegmon, 1992: 517–18). Debate lies in determining what elements of style have cultural meaning, how they convey meaning, and what that cultural meaning is. For a pot, style is conveyed not just by decoration but by the formal choices a potter made during the making of a vessel in vessel morphology and surface treatment.

For the purposes of this Element, we shall be investigating style as is used to define changes in types. The classic example of typological change applied to chronology is W. M. Flinders Petrie's seriation of predynastic pottery (Petrie, 1901, 1899). Petrie showed that predynastic wavy-handled vessels changed from large, shouldered jars with actual wavy handles (the earliest exemplar of the form) to thin, cylindrical vessels with incised lines near the top in lieu of handles (a later manifestation of the form). Seriation provides relative dates and is a durable technique, though today this is done on computer and has moved to statistical analyses (particularly, correspondence analysis: for example, see Bader, 2012).

Seriation shows that stylistic change can be observed through changes in vessel types, affecting the typology. Stylistic change has more than simple chronological utility because style communicates sociocultural information as well as being tied to vessel function and technology (Conkey, 1990: 10–11). Types change due to a complicated cocktail of new trends in the culture, changing production technology, developments in vessel function and application, and shifts in oversight of potters. The population's need for more ceramics at differing frequencies also plays a role, as some types of vessels are broken at greater rates than others. Stylistic change can also result from demand by the population (see Schiestl and Seiler, 2012b: 26, 52–53), reminding us that what appears to be simple diachronic change in a form is actually the result of diachronic shifts within multiple intersecting cultural and social mores.

Our case studies will come from the late Predynastic Period through the Middle Kingdom. This chronological breadth reaches into earlier periods than employed in previous sections, as study of the relationship of social to political change in the Old Kingdom requires that one look to the preceding periods.

4.2 Cultural Consistency at the Dawn of the Egyptian State

The beginning of Pharaonic history includes two major breaking points in the political chronology: the beginning of the Early Dynastic Period, when the first kings of a unified Egypt arose (ca. 3000 BC; see Table 1) and the beginning of the Old Kingdom, when royal mortuary monuments begin to be made of stone (ca. 2686 BC). Yet the ceramic typologies at these points emphasize cultural continuity through seemingly great political change.

Our example comes from the end of the Predynastic Period (Naqada III/ Dynasty 0) and beginning of the Early Dynastic Period (Dynasties 1–2). Pinning this period down chronologically is complex. Accounting for Dynasty 0, the preunification rulers immediately preceding the kings of Dynasty 1, and determining exactly which king unified Upper and Lower Egypt are open issues (see Köhler, 2013: 225–26; Hendrickx, 2006: 88). Dynasties 1 and 2 mark the beginning of dynastic history and also approximate the breaking point between historic and prehistoric Egypt. At this time, the historic chronology of Egypt begins to be applied and Egyptian history begins. The history books start writing of kings and monuments, puzzling out royal administrations, and identifying tombs belonging to the central elite.

A challenge, then, is that the bulk of the evidence for the Early Dynastic Period is archaeological and not historic as scant text dates to the period, especially Dynasty 2 (Köhler, 2013: 225–29). Artifacts, especially ceramics, are therefore crucial for determining both dates and cultural transitions. The ceramic chronology for the period is based on the predynastic ceramic seriation originally established by W. M. Flinders Petrie (1901, 1899), amended by Werner Kaiser (1957), and further corrected by Stan Hendrickx (1996). Today, Hendrickx's Naqada terminology is commonly accepted (see Hendrickx, 2011; Hendrickx, 2006).

But this predynastic seriation is not limited to the Predynastic Period. Following Hendrickx's terminology, Naqada IIIC (and subphases) and IIID equate, respectively, to Dynasties 1 and 2, at least in broad terms (Köhler, 2013: 225; Hendrickx, 2006: tables II.1.6, II.1.7). The ceramics of Naqada IIIC and IIID are, as suggested by the nomenclature, closely linked to the wares and types appearing earlier during the Predynastic Period, with many vessel types continuing to be manufactured during the three periods (Figure 13). Pottery dating to the Early Dynastic Period is difficult to define as specifically Dynastic. The ceramics show no cultural break between prehistoric and dynastic Egypt, with political unification prompting little direct mark on ceramic-related cultural practice and identity. Archaeologists' continued use of predynastic terms such as Naqada IIIC/D when dating the pottery of the Early Dynastic Period makes the link between the two evident in any archaeological publication, though occasionally the application of both a political and an archaeological chronology to the same period can be confusing.

Naqada IIIC/D material is earlier than most of the case studies presented in this Element; however, this period has important bearing on our understanding of Egyptian culture at the beginning of the Old Kingdom. Naqada terminology –

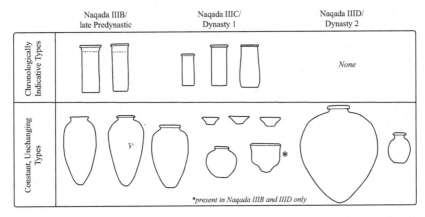

Figure 13 Naqada seriation, with examples of chronologically relevant and irrelevant forms. (drawn by author and Pieter Collet, following data from Hendrickx, 2011: Figure 1; 1989: table 6 and 6.2.1. Vessels from Petrie, 1953: pls. I, II, VIII, IX, XIV; 1921: pls. XXXVIII, L)

referencing a prehistoric, predynastic culture – ceases to be applied to archaeological materials after the end of the Early Dynastic Period. Starting with Dynasty 3, typically taken to mark the beginning of the Old Kingdom, ceramicists date pottery to specific dynasties and refer to an Old Kingdom ceramic corpus. Technological innovations such as the wheel are introduced in this period, though narrowly used by Old Kingdom Egyptians (Doherty, 2015; Bárta, 1995a: 22–24). There is a consistency in type, general shape of the vessels, surface treatments, and technology used in ceramics throughout the Old Kingdom.

Politically, the division from Early Dynastic to Old Kingdom is a bit artificial. Khasekhemwy is the last king to rule in the Early Dynastic Period; his son Djoser the first to rule in the Old Kingdom. Dynasty 3 material is difficult to date via the historic chronology, in part because the kings themselves and their sequencing are so poorly known (Seidlmayer, 2006). In turning to Old Kingdom pottery, that corpus emphasizes the artificialness of this chronological division. The ceramics from Dynasty 3 sites bear a strong resemblance to those from Dynasties 1 and 2 – meaning they show a strong connection to Naqada ceramics and, by extension, Naqada culture (Köhler, 2013: 231; Köhler et al., 2011: 106; Hendrickx, 2006: 87). For example, the late Dynasty 2/Dynasty 3 beer jar with a collared rim was an extension of the "wavy sided" beer jars of Naqada IIID/Dynasty 2 (Köhler's Type 4: Köhler, 2014a: 32, 37; Köhler et al., 2011: 103, 108; see also Hood, 2018: 156, 162). Meidum bowls, discussed above as a common and well-recognized Old Kingdom form, have at least one origin in a deep bowl in Dynasty 2/Naqada IIID (Sterling, 2015: 59; 2009;

Hendrickx et al., 2002; Raue in Kaiser et al., 1999). If one extends analysis into the high Old Kingdom, it becomes evident that versions of both beer jars and Meidum bowls continue well through Dynasty 6, tying the Old Kingdom in an unbroken manner to its predynastic antecedents (Figs. 2.1, 4.3). Naqada culture does not seem to end so much as gradually transform. Yet as archaeologists no longer employ the Naqada chronology after the end of the Early Dynastic Period, the continuity between the three periods easy to lose or ignore (see also Köhler et al., 2011: 106). Nomenclature is important, as it creates categories and structures within which we think. New terms for old ceramic phenomena suggest we should focus on the political changes that mark the dynastic structure rather than on the underlying continuity of Egyptian cultural practices over the fourth and third millennia BC.

Political unification did not result in ceramic revolution. Political unification certainly resulted in the introduction of new, elite forms of art, including statuary, relief, and of course, writing. Elite art changed at these periods as the political bureaucracy shifted and diverted wealth to people based on their relationship to the king. High art is limited in distribution and its raw materials more difficult to come by, making the production of such goods easier to

Figure 14 Dynasty 2 [right] and Dynasty 6 [left] beer jars from Elephantine.
(photos by author)

control. Accordingly, elite statuary, relief, tomb size, jewelry, and other such objects geared to display are well suited for expressing power and authority. Functional objects like ceramics, however, were made of easily accessible material, used by all classes, and ensconced in routine domestic and ritual actions (see Seidlmayer, 2007). By the end of the Predynastic Period, pottery becomes utilitarian and no longer suited for showcasing status or authority, meaning that large-scale ceramic change is less likely to be influenced by political change.

However, elite culture did not include most Egyptians. Even for the elite, high art did not define all cultural activity and the ceramics they used were largely the same as those employed by the lower classes. Pottery, being a low-value good produced by generally low-status individuals, did not form part of the body of material used to proclaim and legitimize the power of the king or the administration. If we think of ceramics as tools used to support different, fundamental, cultural activities (e.g., cooking, ritual, economic exchange), their stability and slow evolution across the late Predynastic through the Old Kingdom strongly indicates that the abrupt change occurring in the political sphere was offset by continuing traditions that changed only gradually, as they always had. Culturally, ceramics suggest that what it was to be Egyptian had solidified long before Dynasty 1 and that this Egyptian identity continued through the Old Kingdom.

More work remains to be done linking the ceramic corpora of these periods together as we endeavor to understand how political unification might have impacted non-elite cultural expression. We must be cautious not to embrace such a task as a monolithic endeavor, for Naqada pottery seems to show regionalism in its use and distribution like that seen in the Old Kingdom (Köhler, 2014b).

4.3 Cultural Continuity Bridging Kingdoms

The historic chronology divides Kingdoms, unified periods ruled by an Egyptian king, from Intermediate Periods, times when the royal house is noncentralized, weak, or foreign. This modern framework implies that the rise and fall of the royal house were major pivot points within the Egyptian past. But as the ceramic record implies a consistency in Egyptian culture with the rise of the royal power, one must correspondingly ask if the twilight of royal power actually resulted in broad cultural change. To examine the result of royal decline on material culture we turn to three historical periods: the late Old Kingdom, the First Intermediate Period, and the early Middle Kingdom (ca. 2686–2055 BC; Table 1). Together these encapsulate the fall and rebirth of unified political power. Though the modern historic nomenclature encourages us to think of these periods as discrete, staccato historical eras, in ancient lived experience they would have been experienced as a continuum.

Historically, the division between the Old Kingdom and the First Intermediate Period is disputed. The Old Kingdom has been taken as ending after the Dynasty 6 reign of Pepi II, though it is more commonly accepted as continuing through Dynasty 8 despite the lack of preserved, large-scale monuments (for example, Seidlmayer, 2006; Warburton et al., 2006: 491; Shaw, 2000: 480). The First Intermediate Period, then, would begin with the advent of Dynasties 9 and 10. The kings of Dynasties 9 and 10 continued to reign from Lower Egypt, with some of its rulers acknowledged in Middle and Upper Egypt (Schneider, 2017, 317; Seidlmayer, 2006: 165–66). Our evidence for the period is splotchy, particularly in Dynasties 9 and 10 and in the delta. The First Intermediate Period's ending is more certain, with political unification of Egypt under Nebhepetre Mentuhotep II marking the beginning of the Middle Kingdom – even though his reign occurs in the middle of Dynasty 11.

Archaeologically and ceramically, the boundaries between the three periods are more difficult to establish firmly. The First Intermediate Period ceramic corpus was an outgrowth of the Old Kingdom ceramic corpus. Ceramic evolution appears to begin its divergence at the end of Dynasty 6, meaning that the First Intermediate Period ceramic corpus begins to form during the end of the Old Kingdom (Seidlmayer, 1990: 395–97). The rate of ceramic change was differential across the country. Old Kingdom types and shapes faded out of use at different times, depending where in the country one analyzes, with Lower Egypt (in this case, meaning the delta south to Beni Hasan) staying closer to Old Kingdom types than Upper Egypt. Within the Lower and Upper Egypt division, sites show differential paces of ceramic evolution emphasizing local differences even in this time. The same type found at, for example, Elephantine, Denderah, and Ayn Asil, were made at different absolute dates (see le Provost, 2016: 365).

Once firmly in the First Intermediate Period, the ceramics are marked by division between ceramics made and used in the north, which tend of have an elongated body shape, and those made and used in the south, which typically have bag-shaped bodies (Figure 15; Seidlmayer, 1990: 348–49). This finding has often been used to support an argument that the First Intermediate Period was a period of regionalization (Section 3.3). As we saw in Section 3, however, regional production and styles were common during the Old Kingdom and before, making the regionalism of the First Intermediate Period different not in concept, but in extent.

The "archaeological First Intermediate Period" does not directly equate to the historic-political First Intermediate Period (Seidlmayer, 2006: note 1; 1990:

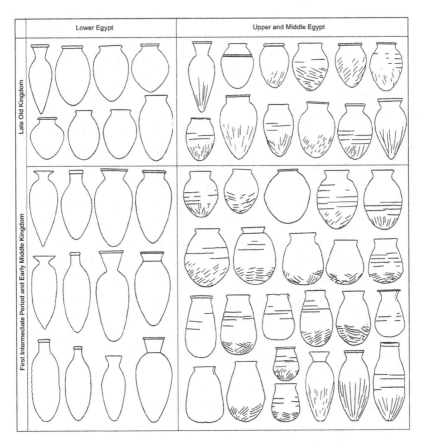

Figure 15 First Intermediate Period jars, morphologically divided between those with elongated bodies (preferred at northern sites) and those with bag-shaped bodies (made and used in the south). (Seidlmayer, 2000: 123; used with permission of Stephan Seidlmayer)

431–42). Thus, pinpointing the end of the First Intermediate Period ceramic corpus is also problematic. Many of the pots that define the Middle Kingdom corpus appear first around Lisht, the early Middle Kingdom royal burial ground, in the reign of Senwosret I. They seem to have remained constrained to the zone of the capital (Arnold, 1988b: 146), at least initially. Meanwhile, the First Intermediate Period-style ceramic corpus continued to be manufactured and used elsewhere in Egypt until the middle of Dynasty 12, many generations after Egypt was politically reunified into the Middle Kingdom (Seidlmayer, 1990: 397). Even the idea of a "First Intermediate Period corpus" and a "Middle Kingdom corpus" is a drastic oversimplification as some of the key forms one might consider markers of the Middle Kingdom – hemispherical cups, cylindrical bread molds (Figures 11, 17) – were either introduced in the First Intermediate Period or had First Intermediate Period antecedents (Warden, 2019; Schiestl and Seiler, 2012a: 84, 750). However, the Middle Kingdom ceramic corpus includes none of the major types of the Old Kingdom (Seidlmayer, 1990: 432).

Yet some ceramic types were continually produced across all three periods, marking cultural consistency. One example is the bread plate (Figure 16; Marchand, 2017: 227–29). This common form used to produce bread was first introduced in Dynasty 5 as the *aperet* (Egyptian: ꜥprt) mold (Bárta, 1995b). It is so ubiquitous throughout the third and early second millennia BC and often so poorly preserved in the archaeological record that the type is useless for dating. Its popularity across time and space highlights a continuity of cultural practice across Egypt, particularly within the sphere of subsistence and cooking.

Simultaneously, changing ceramic types suggests that the First Intermediate Period yielded new economic structures that had long-term ramifications. Bread and beer had been fundamental payments for labor in the Old Kingdom; the archaeological record preserves abundant evidence for this exchange in ceramic beer jars and *bedja* bread molds, ubiquitous at any Old Kingdom site (Warden, 2014: 97–99, 140–45). Beer jars, though, are an early casualty of the ceramic change, no longer appearing after Dynasty 6 (Warden, 2020: 1633–34). Instead, they were replaced by numerous jar forms of the First Intermediate Period, all seemingly multiuse forms and none intended specifically for beer. As a result, beer exchange would no longer have been easy to visually verify. The commodity was probably no longer treated as a basic exchange good and so no longer needed to be easily identifiable.

Bread molds fare a bit differently. The *bedja* form appears to lose popularity beginning with the close of Dynasty 6. Yet bread molds do not categorically

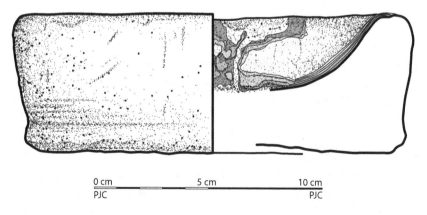

0 cm   5 cm   10 cm
PJC   PJC

Figure 16 Example of a "bread plate" or *aperet* mold. (drawn by Pieter Collet)

disappear. Rather, the form changes. Elephantine provides a good example. After Dynasty 6, *bedja* molds with heavy walls, thick bases, and wide diameter stop being used in favor of a medium-thick walled, flat-based mold with a rim diameter about half the *bedja*'s size. This transition is accomplished late in the Old Kingdom (Warden, 2019; Raue, 2018b: 194–95). As the First Intermediate Period progressed, molds became conical, reducing further in diameter and wall thickness. The narrowing, thinning trend continues into the Middle Kingdom, becoming the cylindrical mold common in the Middle Kingdom corpus (Fig 4.6; Warden, 2019; Jacquet-Gordon, 1981: 11–19). The loaves baked in these molds were likely used as wage payments throughout these centuries, following an economic structure established at least in as early as the Old Kingdom and found in Middle Kingdom textual records (Warden, 2019, 2014; Mueller, 1975).

The Middle Kingdom's new loaf types were not the result of a new centralized government, but rather First Intermediate Period practice. It was in the First Intermediate Period that mold size shrank and baking practices changed. The new, smaller, thinner First Intermediate Period mold did not simply arise from aesthetic interest or chronological trends. Such changes were entangled with changes in pottery production, the baking industry, and technological shifts affecting economic exchange. When the Middle Kingdom arose, the new central government did not result in a strong change of bread production. The form was modified in slight ways, becoming smaller in diameter and thinner-walled, changes that were logical extensions of the mode of production already introduced in the First Intermediate Period. The continuity in the form is particularly meaningful when we remember the fundamental economic role of bread. By leaving bread molds well enough alone, basic economic exchange is not impacted by recentralization of

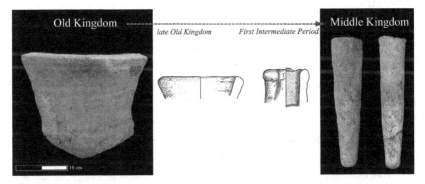

Figure 17 Example of bread mold change from Old to Middle Kingdoms. Examples from Elephantine. (photos by author; drawings by Pieter Collet)

government. Rather, cultural and economic practices from a period of government fragmentation continued. As this one form shows, at least some aspects of the Middle Kingdom ceramic corpus and the social structures underpinning it were extensions of the social changes occurring during the First Intermediate Period.

4.4 Conclusion

Typological study of ceramics shows that the historical/political boundaries presented in most Egyptian histories have little bearing on social or cultural change, whose boundaries, when they exist at all, are often fuzzy. This is true at the dawn of the Egyptian state, when the ceramics show an unbroken cultural line progressing from the prehistoric Naqada Periods through the Early Dynastic Period and further into the early Old Kingdom. It is true for the divisions between the Old Kingdom, First Intermediate Period, and Middle Kingdom, when central political power first fell and was recreated while economic activity within sites was managed outside of the fortunes of the crown. The cessation of production of Old Kingdom style pots, and later the rise of Middle Kingdom-style manufacture, shows temporal and spatial fluctuation perhaps in part due to regional relationships, differential reliance or interaction with central power, and different local identities. Even in the Middle Kingdom, change in ceramic types and frequencies occurs at differential rates within one site (Bourriau and Gallorini, 2016: 207). Clean breaks in the ceramic corpus do not exist and change is gradual, ultimately meaning that political history will not, and for the most part cannot, bear a one-to-one relationship with material culture. Ceramic corpora do not show clean breaks; rather, much like human culture, they reflect both what has just passed as well as present concerns. Cultural change was not limited to political boundaries because the rise and fall of the kingship was only one part of the complicated web that supported Egyptian culture.

5 The Complexity of Private Life

"Private life" is used here as an umbrella term to encompass Egyptian identity and lived experience, particularly in this case nonroyal individuals. I deliberately avoid the term "daily life" because, as used in Egyptology, it encodes a smaller range of activity boiling down to habitual, daily actions. "Private life" expands the scope of investigation to social life, identity, and self-conception in line with the greater concerns of social archaeology. Private life sits in opposition to the idea of the afterlife. Both deal with ideology, belief, and identity. The afterlife, though, is tied to issues of memorialization and remembrance that give it the weight of permanence. Tombs, their art, and their contents are idealized to sit in accord with the ideological needs of eternity. Private life, on the other hand, was fluid and constantly changing: a short, passing experience spent within mudbrick walls and on changing agricultural fields. The fundamental challenges of food production and community building that dominated lived experience were met through activities employing objects of low intrinsic value but high utility. Material culture was thus an active constituent of private life and pottery an essential element of the toolkit.

The intended permanence of the Egyptian tomb renders any application of mortuary data to private life theoretically complex. People lived in settlements; settlements are accordingly the logical place to turn to reconstruct private *life*. Perhaps more importantly for this Element, however, is the fact that settlement archaeology in Egypt is an expanding but still underworked field (for overviews: Moeller, 2016; Snape, 2014). A tremendous volume of ceramic material comes from settlement excavation. These sherds – and only rarely complete pots – often await extended analyses.

The ever-changing nature of Egyptian settlements present archaeological challenges. Houses were built of mudbrick and intended to be used, expanded, torn down, and rebuilt. Settlements themselves were located near the Nile, in or near the inundated land, to allow access to agricultural fields and water. As a result, outside of exceptional circumstances (e.g., Tell el-Amarna), ancient neighborhoods and houses do not come to us well-preserved or easy to interpret. Their stratigraphy is jumbled by pits, dumps, and leveling activity. Ancient towns are often under or near modern towns, making them particularly challenging to excavate as the needs of the present and the past collide.

Like settlement architecture, domestic objects, too, were always in flux and not intended to last forever. Pots were broken and the resultant pieces made into circular tokens, tools, ostraca, or even used to make new mudbricks. Stone tools were retouched, broken, and discarded. Further, artifacts were portable and intended to move over the course of their life. Rarely do archaeologists find objects in the place of their actual use (*in situ*). Houses were used until they were rebuilt or abandoned; when that occurred, families took their objects to the new dwelling instead of leaving the old space intact. As a result, the bulk of the material culture of private life is preserved in domestic dumps likely representing the detritus of several households over a long period, discarded in a manner perhaps unrelated to their use or meaning. Accordingly, function and who used what are not always clear in settlement contexts.

Human life is dynamic but the archaeological record hands us still frames, the dynamic made static and fractured. The simple abundance of settlement ceramics implies their centrality to social action and social identity. Our methods can help us move from static object to dynamic life processes. This section will focus on two elements of private life: ethnic identity and domestic activity. These foci encourage us to move from large theoretical space to fine grained detail, identity to lived practice. However, identity did not – does not – exist in a vacuum and is not fully encapsulated into one artifact or artifact type. Any ceramic study of private life will be enriched by working with specialists in other datasets (such as lithics, linen, botany, zooarchaeology, and biological anthropology, to name a few) and analyses.

5.1 Theories and Methods

First we will approach corporate identity through the lens of ethnicity: a nonbiological corporate identity that uses as its base an idea of shared origin, shared language, and shared ideology to create an in-group. Ethnic identity is self-defined, fluid, and performed (Moreno García, 2018: 1–2; Schneider, 2010: 144; Jones, 1997: 56–105). It is also "mutable and socially contingent" (Smith, 2018: 116). The concept of ethnicity entered the discussion in anthropological archaeology with real force in the 1990s, though it has always been challenging to identify in the material record because of its mutability (Jones, 1997). However, objects are instrumental in performing habitual actions, helping to define ethnicity by enabling and constructing the lived practices that make ethnicity visible (Smith, 2018; Antonaccio, 2010; Jones, 1997: 92–94, 120–23). Material culture seen in this light is an active constituent of ethnic identity.

Recent discussions of ethnicity in the archaeological record have been informed by theories about how people and cultures interact, blend, and identify. Ideas of cultural assimilation and cultural diffusion continue to be employed. At the same time, the literature has expanded to think about ethnicity as actively constructed through complex processes including cultural hybridization, when a new ethnicity arises from the merger of two or more (similar to "mixity"); and creolization, where select elements from one group are absorbed by another, typically without the original cultural connotations and with large power differentials between groups (Moreno García, 2018: 6–7; Gatto, 2014: 97; Bader, 2013: 261–63; Antonaccio, 2010: 36, 45; for ceramic challenges Braun, 2016: 70–71; 2005: 145). These processes can be understood to fall under the greater umbrella of entanglement, which asserts that objects influence people, who in turn influence objects, and so on, resulting in identities – including ethnic identities – that were messy and intertwined rather than simplistic and categorical (Smith, 2018; Pelt, 2013; Hodder, 2012: 88–97). Clearly these approaches ignore ethnicity as personal feeling or individual self-definition (see Knapp, 2014: 35–36), as the archaeological record tends to speak more to actions than to beliefs, to corporate practice rather than individual experience.

It is not uncommon to find multiple terms expressing ethnic relationships used in the same article (e.g., Raue, 2019). These processes coexisted and no single term provides a complete explanation for how cultures interact and new ethnic identities formed. As ethnicity is neither bounded or "pure," it must always be understood in its archaeological context, requiring archaeologists to consider provenience and intended audience when making interpretations (Antonaccio, 2010: 38; Jones, 1997: 100–04). Obviously, ceramics are not the only material to be brought to identifying ethnicities, and ethnic identities in Egypt have been studied through art, text, and monument. Our ceramic case studies expand these discussions and underscore the daily, lived complexity of ethnicity. Some reference to New Kingdom material will also allow us to round out our discussion of ethnicity vis-à-vis the ceramic record; these are included because they provide good examples of important approaches informative in further thinking about earlier material.

For the second half of this section we shall approach household activities by looking at vessel function and use. Egyptian vessels appear to have been multifunctional and their intended use poorly defined. To interpret their actual use and thus the vessels' actual domestic roles, our case studies employ experimental archaeology. Experimental archaeology calls for the use of modern experiments to deduce possible interpretations of the material record. To provide a model of what ancient activity looked like the experiment must be carried out in conditions as akin to those available in the past, often meaning that they are *not* conducted in the lab or in a sterile environment. The more parallel the conditions the better the experimental data for the purposes of archaeological interpretation. As a result, archaeologists try to replicate as closely as possible materials, techniques, and settings identified in the archaeological record when establishing the parameters of an experiment. In Egyptian ceramic studies, experiments have expanded our understanding of topics such as firing technology (Nicholson, 1995; Soukiassian et al., 1990) and wheel manufacture (Doherty, 2015: 82–90). This section focuses particularly on the use of experimental archaeology to determining possible vessel function, as function helps us approached mundane, lived experiences (Rice, 1987: 211).

5.2 Who Were They? Identity, Ethnicity, and Ceramics

As commonly employed, the term "Egyptian" is a shorthand, using location and government to define ethnic identity in a self-referential loop. Egyptian elite art often presents a standardized image of ancient Egyptians marked by skin color, hair style, dress, and other accoutrements. The ethnic "other" – Libyans, Nubians,

Levantine peoples (often termed "Asiatics") – were marked in similar manners (Smith, 2007: 218–29). These images convey a sense of created order and hierarchy in the social world and provide an ideologically potent *topos* supporting Egyptian royal power and authority – not to mention Egyptian ethnocentrism (Smith, 2014: 196, 2003b; Loprieno, 1988). Yet most of Egypt was open in some way to the foreign. The deserts, the cataracts, and the seas provide daunting yet permeable barriers through which both ideas and people regularly moved (see also Bárta, 2010). The whole country was a border, with all sites providing points of contact with others where identity might be mediated and integrated. Thus, this discussion expands from above discussion of regional interaction between Egypt and foreigners (Section 3.4) to explore how intermingling might have helped build ethnic identities. Accordingly, Egyptian ethnicity probably had local and regional expressions (Schneider, 2010: 145; Newman, 2003: 17; Baines, 1996: 36). Individual actors might have challenged and shifted their own ethnic identity, presenting differently when socially advantageous or ideologically required (Smith, 2018: 116–17, 125, 129; 2014: 207).

At the most basic, one begins to identify ethnic display by identifying patterns of difference in the material record. The strongest indicators of lived ethnic difference are large-scale patterns that encompass multiple elements of the material record. Patterns limited to one artifact type, such as pottery, can be explained through many mechanisms, such a simple trade. However, when patterns of difference encompass multiple elements of material culture – for example, pottery, graves, weapons, bodies (e.g., Schrader et al., 2018; Redmount, 1995) – the argument for ethnic differentiation becomes more compelling. This is not to say that one element of material culture *cannot* indicate ethnic difference, but rather that difference as expressed through multiple artifact types suggests that ethnic difference was clearly demarcated and practiced by the ancient community. With that noted, we shall turn to explore ethnicity particularly through the ceramic record, with the knowledge that any ceramicist carrying out such work must also interact with the broader archaeological record and with other specialists to draw a full picture.

Many of the studies of ethnicity in Egypt of the Old through Middle Kingdoms have focused on the extreme south (the first Upper Egyptian nome through Lower Nubia) or the northeast (the eastern Nile Delta through the southern Levant).[5] The western border and its presumed connections with Libya have been little studied, at least during these periods (though see Hope, 2007). Thus, our below case studies will focus on the eastern Delta and First

[5] Though see Schneider 2010: 149–51 for nonceramic, statewide overview of "foreigners" in Egypt.

Cataract. Sites in these areas illuminate the porosity of the Egyptian border, demonstrating that state borders did not dictate private life in the Egyptian past.

5.3 Egyptians and the Peoples of the Levant

During the late fourth and early third millennia, it has often been posited that Egyptians colonized portions of the southern Levant based in part on the appearance of large quantities of sherds of Egyptian types, manufacture, or fabrics known to come from the Nile Valley (e.g., Tell Sakan: de Miroschedji and Sadeq, 2005; for overview of Egyptian colonization of the Levant: Wengrow, 2006: 89, 137–40). Colonial sites are ripe for studies of ethnicity as the colonial endeavor guarantees the close proximity of two or more ethnic groups: in this case, Egyptian and Levantine. How and where different styles of material culture manifested has the potential to document ethnic identity and relationships between ethnic groups. Unfortunately, even the act of applying nomenclature leads us into making problematic assumptions. For example: in the Levant of the late fourth millennium, vessels that are of Egyptian form are typically called "Egyptian" and are taken as documenting an Egyptian presence in the area. The remainder of the corpus is indigenous in style and manufacture and thus called "Levantine."

Though it might be clichéd, pots are not people. The terms "Egyptian" and "Levantine" as used above are based on form and technology of the vessels' manufacture. By quantifying a large number of pots under the nomer "Egyptian," a simple equation is created between a vessel type and the ethnicity of the individual who made or used the pot (Braun, 2016: 69). Egyptian presence in the Levant seems large when ethnicity is equated with vessel type. Eliot Braun has suggested that a more complex terminological toolkit be used, based not just on type and manufacture but on fabric. As raw material does not seem to have been traded, any vessel made of Egyptian fabric was made in Egypt, and those of Levantine fabrics made in the Levant. Accordingly, Braun applies the terms "Egyptianizing" to vessels that follow Egyptian typology but was manufactured in the Levant. "Southern Levantinizing" is used for vessels of southern Levantine types manufactured in Egypt, known at multiple sites during the Early Dynastic Period (Wilkinson, 2002: 516–17). He reserves the terms "Egyptian" for Egyptian-style vessels made in Egypt and "southern Levantine" for vessels southern Levantine-type vessels made in the southern Levant (Braun, 2016: 70). Though the changed terminology might feel cumbersome, it successfully uncouples pots from ethnic terms and assumptions, instead marking the derivation of form and manufacture. It also changes the quantification of ceramics as instead of two categories there are four. What might have seemed as large-scale Egyptian presence in colonies due to the presence of a large number of Egyptian might be re-problematized as Egyptian influence resulting in a large number of Egyptianizing vessels manufactured locally in the Levant. These terms provide space for productive discussion about who was where and how stylistic influences might move across borders and through cultures.

The picture becomes fuller over a thousand years later, during the Middle Kingdom. This time, the point of contact was the Egyptian eastern Delta, at the site of Tell el-Dab'a. During the Middle Kingdom, Tell el-Dab'a was a constant point of contact between Egypt and the southern Levant. In the early Middle Kingdom, Tell el-Dab'a had been in regular trade with the northern Levant, receiving trade goods in Levantine vessels. At the same time, Tell el-Dab'a's potters also made some southern Levantinizing, Canaanite forms (Cohen-Weinberger and Goren, 2004: 82–83, table 3). By the late Middle Kingdom, Levantinizing pots, perfectly Levantine in form and production but Egyptian in fabric, begin to be made in large quantities on-site – in the late Middle Kingdom (late Dynasty 12–13) making up 20 percent of the settlement assemblage and 90 percent of ceramics from mortuary contexts (Bietak, 1997: 91). Contemporary to these sherds were other Levantinizing material culture, including burials and domestic architecture (Bader, 2013: 266, 270–71, 275; Aston, 2004/2: 91–179, 194–97; Bietak, 1997: 97–105). Over time, the ceramics show a blending of Egyptian and southern Levantine traits to form a distinct local ethnicity that would become Hyksos culture (Aston, 2004). Bader suggests that we view the resultant mixture as a creolization, a merger of different ethnicities into something new (2013: 262, 277–78). It should be noted that the ceramics and other finds speak remarkably well to shifting ethnic identities precisely because they have been quantified, compared to materials from other Egyptian and southern Levantine sites, and fully analyzed according to their provenience.

The new Hyksos material culture set dominated Tell el-Dab'a, its ethnic center, but also appears to have spread throughout the eastern Delta (Rzepka et al., 2017: 40–41; Redmount, 1995). However, considering the power of the Hyksos in the Second Intermediate Period, it is an odd quirk that the new material culture is not found in the Nile Valley, not even in Memphis (Bader, 2013: 273). Perhaps it was not expedient to appear ethnically Hyksos outside of the eastern Delta heartland. Hyksos individuals who did move south perhaps showcased an Egyptian ethnic identity when they did so. Such would accord with the Hyksos scarabs and texts of the time, which employed Egyptian script and iconography, presumably because these Egyptian ethnic markers encoded legitimate power in the Nile Valley.

5.4 Egyptians and Nubians

Nomenclature is similarly important in studying Egypt's southern border with Nubia. Here, pottery is often called "Egyptian" or "Nubian." However, the problems inherent in equating pottery types with ethnic groups is rarely addressed in this context and these simple identifiers of style can slide into interpretations of bounded ethnicity (e.g., Hafsaas, 2006–07). Cultural attribution is further exacerbated by the common identification of specific Nubian groups with specific ceramic types, problematically defining those groups to objects in such a way as to potentially misidentify or reify different Nubian peoples (Raue, 2012). For Nubian and Egyptian ceramic material, terminology is difficult to move to geographical, manufacture-based terms. Pots made in Nubia or Egypt are commonly made of clays deposited by the Nile, whose visual characteristics are very similar regardless of whether the clay came from Egypt or Nubia. Thus, we cannot divide the "Egyptian" from the "Egyptianizing" clearly, nor the "Nubian" from the "Nubianizing." Here, I will use the neutral terms "Egyptian-style" and "Nubian-style" to describe material from ethnically mixed contexts in order not to presuppose ethnic markers. As Nubians themselves were a diverse community of different groups, this discussion includes a degree of simplification to focus broadly on the dynamics of cultural relationships.

Much of the work on the entanglement of Egyptian and Nubian ethnicities has taken place at Egyptian colonial sites within Nubia itself: fortresses, towns, and tombs that were built by the Egyptians beginning in the Middle Kingdom as they sought to control Lower Nubia and beyond. The ceramic corpora of these sites followed the stylistic and technological trends found in Egypt proper. Even the fabric of these pots emulated that found in Egyptian-made vessels, including the same types and amounts of temper (e.g., Smith, 2003b: 94). While it is impossible to be certain if these Egyptian-style vessels were manufactured in Nubia or Egypt due to challenges in separating Nile clay material visually, the quantity of ceramic material would make local manufacture the most likely. The sheer volume of Egyptian-style pots at Egyptian colonial sites in Nubia shows that the people who lived there in the Middle Kingdom actively partook of Egyptian cultural practices when cooking and serving. The townspeople likely distributed their goods following to Egyptian cultural patterns – at least, we can posit that for any goods traded in ceramic vessels, as storage vessels (presumably also used for transportation) were Egyptian in form (Smith, 2018: 134–36). They deliberately displayed and performed Egyptian ethnicity. Were they all of Egyptian extraction? That is a different, and perhaps unanswerable, question. The majority population, however, performed Egyptian ethnicity.

Nubian-style material forms a portion of the corpus as well: mostly utilitarian pottery, particularly cooking wares. This distribution is particularly evident at Askut, where in the Middle Kingdom Nubian-style wares composed 40 percent of the cooking vessel corpus, while less than 5 percent of the table ware ceramics were Nubian-style (Smith, 2018: 134, fig. 7). The volume of Nubian-style cooking vessels suggests that Nubian cooking practices were common, perhaps indicating the presence of Nubians in colonial kitchens (Smith, 2003a, 2003b: 192–93). Food preparation, then, was one avenue where Nubian ethnicity could be displayed at Askut (Smith, 2018: 135–36). The remaining 60 percent of the cooking ware corpus was Egyptian style, suggesting a hybrid approach to cuisine and food production that took elements from both cultures and merged them. The balance displayed changed over time as Nubian political power recovered in Lower Nubia (Smith, 2018: 135–37). Similar multiethnic practices are seemingly signaled at the colonial cemetery of Tombos (dating to the New Kingdom), which yielded a mixture of Egyptian-style and Nubian-style burials containing artifacts of both Egyptian and Nubian cultural adherence (Smith, 2018: 137–39). Some tombs' material culture overwhelmingly signaled Nubian ethnic status, further suggesting that there was less interest in displaying Egyptian-ness in a New Kingdom funerary context than there was in the lived, colonial settlements of the Middle Kingdom. Whether that was due to shifting dynamics from life to death, or Middle to New Kingdom, certainly the balance of ethnic display suggests the desirability of an ethnicity, and the ability to express it, had both diachronic and life-and-death ramifications.

Nubian-style material in Egypt is most notable within the first Upper Egyptian nome. This area was rife with Nubian-style material culture. Perhaps it is best to understand this nome as part of the cultural geography of Nubia rather than a component of the Egyptian cultural homeland, for all that it was always considered part of the Egyptian state (Raue, 2018a; Gatto, 2005). The settlement at Elephantine, right at the traditional border between Egypt and Nubia, presents a picture where Nubian influence and existence cannot be ignored. Nubian-style sherds are common, though numerically scant, throughout Old and Middle Kingdom contexts at the site (Raue, 2018a: 142–73; 2018b: 220–31; M.-K. Schröder, personal communication). Most of these are utilitarian wares commonly assumed to have been used for cooking.

Anthropologically it is accepted that cooking ceramics are conservative; they change more slowly than fine wares because they are tied to the slow change of cooking practices. Food is a basic ingredient of ethnic identity. Cooking practices display ethnic identity inside the house, within intimate space; that identity might not have been performed outside of the home in spaces that were much more public but was just as much an effective marker of ethnic identity (Hodder, 1982: 55–57). It is possible that Nubian-style cooking pots were used by Nubian women married to Egyptian men, as was suggested for Akyut, as cooking in both Egyptian and Nubian cultures is posited to have been gendered female (Smith, 2003a, 2003b: 192–93). Alternately, perhaps Egyptian-style and Nubian-style vessels formed one coherent ethnic unit, fused or entangled into a new, local subculture (Budka, 2016: 290). Regardless, the commonality of Nubian sherds on the island underlines how Elephantine sat at an ethnic junction (Raue, 2008: 3–5). Interaction with Nubian ethnicity was regular, a constant, and perhaps an entangled component of the ethnic identity of those who lived on the island.

At Askut and Elephantine both, the dominant material culture was Egyptian-style, suggesting that these frontier-people chose to publicly express an Egyptian-esque ethnic identity. This ethnic display was perhaps selected by the participants so that they might actively partake in the political power controlling the region. This requires that we think of Egyptian ethnic identity as a construction and not a given, a creation tied to a justification of Egyptian political power (Gatto, 2014: 114–15; see also Baines, 1996: 361). The performance of Egyptian ethnicity itself becomes a statement of alignment, especially in the first Upper Egyptian nome where Nubian material culture forms a constant background noise. The actors who employed this show of Egyptianness might have been of Nubian or Egyptian descent.

5.5 The Domestic Sphere

Ethnic identity was (and is) negotiated in the domestic sphere, particularly the kitchen. Food production provides a place where ethnic identity might be negotiated and expressed privately to intimate circles. The home thus serves as an interface between ideology, practical necessity, and personal choice; individual identity comes into play in how these forces are navigated. Those choices become part of household practice.

In using ceramics to investigating household practices, understanding how pots were used is key. Household ceramics were largely dedicated to food storage, production, and consumption, allowing us to understand how food was cached and cooked within the domestic setting. Such use analyses require the collection of a range of quantifiable ceramic data.

5.5.1 Data Collection

Quantitative data collection and research is a slow process, slower even than the excavation of a site, and analysis of finds frequently lags at least a season or two after their excavation. Data collection is guided by the research questions formulated before work begins Additional questions will arise once data analysis begins and patterns become apparent (Bader, 2016: 48). Thus, I address methodology here because it is fundamental to the questions we ask and can answer (see also Bourriau, 2010: 1–10). Methodology is almost the entirety of fieldwork. Yet despite its basic importance, there is little enough to this point published in Egyptian archaeological spheres.

The form we use for ceramic data collection for the Kom el-Hisn Provincialism Project provides an example of how data may be prioritized and collected (Figure 18). It is very similar to that we use on the Realities of Life Project, Elephantine.[6] Our research questions at both sites address how ceramics were used in cooking and relationships of different ceramic forms within the assemblage and reflect domestic economy and social networks. These data build into studying social and economic relationships and how they might have changed across time and space. These questions require large-scale data collection in order to build robust statistical analyses. Accordingly, we count and weigh sherds in every category in the figure. I expect distribution of wares to yield useful data to the questions, as well as data from specific forms such as bread molds. As a result, we record all sherds, whether diagnostic or from the vessel's body. Data collection and analysis is still ongoing, so findings are preliminary.

Quantification illustrates the realities of lived experience at both settlements. At both sites, the dominant ceramic ware at settlements was coarse and utilitarian (Figure 19, 20). As this finding is common at two sites distant in both time and space, it suggests that coarse wares should be understood as a dominant part of all Egyptian settlement corpora. The dominance of coarse wares is most marked in Old Kingdom Kom el–Hisn (Figure 19). At late Middle Kingdom Elephantine, coarse wares form less of the corpus, though still the majority.

It is clear in this case that accounting for amount varies whether one uses count of sherds or weight of sherds (Figure 20). Weights are the most statistically significant figure of the two as it bears the firmest relationship to actual vessels. Fine wares are thin-walled and particularly prone to breakage, making them overrepresented in sherd counts, while coarse vessels are underrepresented in sherd counts as any small coarse sherds tend to disintegrate. In theory,

---

[6] Kom el-Hisn is excavated as the Kom el-Hisn Provincialism Project (Roanoke College), directed by the present author. The Elephantine concession is held jointly by the German Archaeological Institute (DAI) and the Swiss Institute for Architectural and Archaeological Research on Ancient Egypt; the present author serves as the Head of Ceramics group for the "Realities of Life," subproject, directed by Dr. Johanna Sigl (DAI). Both projects operate with permission of the Egyptian Ministry of Tourism and Antiquities.

Note anything interesting in the comment field, such as type of decoration, placement of cream slip, bm lining, etc

Ware	Surface	Normal	Fire in	Fire out	Fire in/out	Rims tstc	Other (decorated, comments, etc)
Coarse (NS I)	Unslipped						
	R slip in						
	R slip out						
	R slip in/out						
	Other slip						
Medium (NS II+)	Unslipped						
	R slip in						
	R slip out						
	R slip in/out						
	Other slip						
Fine (NS II+)	Unslipped						
	R slip in						
	R slip out						
	R slip in/out						
	Other slip						
NS V	Unslipped						
MI	Unslipped						
MII	Unslipped						

LOCUS NUMBER: Processed by: Date: Page _____ of _____

Figure 18 Ceramic data collection form, Kom el-Hisn.

Type:	Fabric:	Description:		
	Slip:		1)	
			2)	
	Black:		3)	
			4)	
	Addtnl:		5)	
		Object number concordance (photo'd)	*Diameter/percentage/weight*	*Comments*

Type:	Fabric:	Description:		
	Slip:		1)	
			2)	
	Black:		3)	
			4)	
	Addtnl:		5)	
		Object number concordance (photo'd)	*Diameter/percentage/weight*	*Comments*

Type:	Fabric:	Description:		
	Slip:		1)	
			2)	
	Black:		3)	
			4)	
	Addtnl:		5)	
		Object number concordance (photo'd)	*Diameter/percentage/weight*	*Comments*

Type:	Fabric:	Description:		
	Slip:		1)	
			2)	
	Black:		3)	
			4)	
	Addtnl:		5)	
		Object number concordance (photo'd)	*Diameter/percentage/weight*	*Comments*

LOCUS NUMBER:	Processed by:	Date:	Page ____ of ____

Figure 18 Cont.

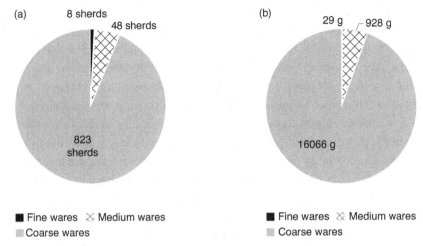

Figure 19 Ware distribution from sample context from Kom el-Hisn (Unit G10.1, early-mid Old Kingdom). Count distribution to left, weight distribution at right. (chart by author)

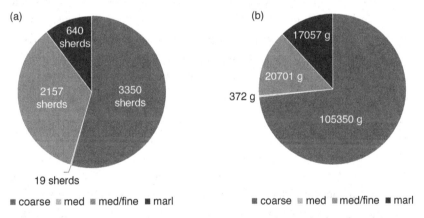

Figure 20 Ware distribution from sample context from Elephantine. (context 46501B/b, late Middle Kingdom; chart by author)

whether the pot is broken into 2 sherds or 200, the totality will always weigh the same amount (Orton and Hughes, 2013: 206–08). EVES – estimated vessel equivalents, a way of quantifying diagnostic sherds based on the amount of the rim or base preserved – are inapplicable here as both projects work largely with body sherds (Orton and Hughes, 2013; Bader, 2010). However, preservation data are collected for all diagnostic sherds should future researchers desire to run eves figures.

The dominance of coarse wares in these two settlement assemblages is not surprising to those with experience in the sherd yard. However, the weight of ceramic publication has been biased toward fine wares, foreign wares, and those that are chronologically indicative. The result is that the normal corpus has not been presented as normal in publication. Quantification of the ceramic data provides information on presence and absence of ceramic wares that influences how we think of Egyptian production activities. Armed with this information we might better hone our research questions. For example, any study of private life should necessarily put its primary focus on the utilitarian wares that made up the bulk of the corpus with which the Egyptians would have interacted. As both the projects at Kom el-Hisn and Elephantine move forward we are putting utilitarian wares as the center of our analyses in hopes that we can understand how they contributed to and informed social practice.

In collecting fine-grained quantitative data, the data are likely to show unanticipated relationships and spur new research questions, and indeed we have collected a wealth of data that we have only begun to analyze. Today, it seems sensible to start thinking of ceramic data as big data and to approach the world of business intelligence and data scientists to think through ways ceramic data might be stored, queried, and visualized. As most archaeologists do not have these technical skills, it behooves us to both build relationships with those computer people who do, to encourage students to go into archaeological computing, and to employ said students once they are done.

5.5.2 Experimental Archaeology

Understanding vessel function allows us to approach how pots were used and how they enabled social activity. Most Egyptian vessels were multifunctional, with a trend to greater functional generalization beginning in the late Early Dynastic Period and continuing to the Middle Kingdom. Residue analysis might help us determine individual vessel function, but to date such studies have rarely been conducted in Egypt due to logistical challenges (though see Khalifa and Elrahim, 2020) and only limited residue analysis has been done on Egyptian vessels in museums (particularly regarding wine: Guasch Jané et al., 2004; McGovern, 1997).

Experimental archaeology can help build a detailed understanding of vessel manufacture, function, and lifespan, even for vessels whose role in production is ostensibly clear. One example is recreation of Middle Kingdom cylindrical bread molds at Ayn Sukhna. While it was evident that this form was used to bake bread, how the vessel was manufactured and used were unknown. Experiments by Adeline Bats, based on Middle Kingdom Ayn Sukhna vessels, aimed to test mold manufacturing processes including the type of temper and potential formation of the mold around a core (Bats, 2017). These experiments further highlighted that the molds did not need to be broken to remove the bread – an assumption informally accepted at many Egyptian archaeological sites. The bread shrunk during the baking process, allowing it to be removed easily (Bats, 2017). Bread was particularly easy to remove when the mold's interior was lined with a fine clay as commonly seen on Middle Kingdom bread mold sherds in the archaeological record (Bats, 2020: 9). The identification of the lining as nonslip accords well with findings at Elephantine where examples of molds with multiple instances of relining are common (Warden, 2019). The Ayn Sukhna experiments show that bread molds could be reused many times, perhaps providing a partial explanation for why there are so few bread molds in some Middle Kingdom settlements (for example, Warden, 2019; Bourriau and Gallorini, 2016: 3–4).

At Elephantine, in trying to understand cooking on the island the ceramic team has been documenting where there are black marks, or entire blackening, on a sherd – inside, outside, or on both surfaces. We aim to determine how sherds may be used to answer questions of use, as many forms in the settlement corpus cannot be fully reconstructed and complete vessels are lacking (though see Skibo, 2013: 106). Exterior blackening marks were presumed to be the result of use on a cooking fire. Interior black marks could be produced by perhaps from turning a vessel upside down on a fire, employing it as a lamp, or from charring food (Skibo, 2013: 87). When sherds from the late Middle Kingdom strata of R07 were analyzed by blackening pattern, 56.6 percent were found to show blackening on some surface (Figure 21). Though this figure is not broken down by ware, it should be noted that all wares showed external and internal blackening. Rarely was this blackening actually sooting that covered the entire exterior or interior surface of the sherd. This accords with the ethnographic record, which shows examples of cooking vessels to often have symmetrical, patchy blackening patterns due to repetitive use and rotation during cooking rather than complete blackening over the surface (Skibo, 2013: 87).

How does the positioning of black spots relate to a Middle Kingdom pot's placement on the fire, types of heat and application, and foodstuffs (see also Rzeuska, 2013: 83)? To determine potential answers for our questions we created our own cooking fire, following the pattern of the fires found in Elephantine houses: a fire directly on the floor's surface, no more than one or two centimeters below walking level. The fire and the experimental vessels were as analogous to the ancient examples as possible. For example, the fire was built of acacia and goat dung (the latter as a substitute for donkey dung). Several modern, unglazed vessels of local clay from the nearby village were filled with water, rice, eggs, or fish and then placed into the fire in different locations: deep into the fire, at its edge, beside the fire. Vessels were also placed in different

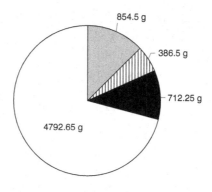

854.5 g

386.5 g

712.25 g

4792.65 g

☐ black in ☐ black out ■ black in/out ☐ none

Figure 21 Corpus of sherds from House 169, R07, late Middle Kingdom contexts. Divided by presence and location of blackening marks. (chart by author)

proximity to the coals: directly on the coals or perched above them on informal tripods of mudbrick fragments (Figure 22).

Three days of cooking over the open fire showed that black marks rarely arose on cooking vessels simply because they were directly submerged into the flames. Strong blackening patterns came from contact with poorly controlled flames or from fats burned off foods. On the first day, many vessels gained blackening marks from poorly contained flames; however, the flames were less hot than the coals and unproductive for cooking. The second day, we placed the pots on the fire after the flames died down. This allowed the pots to be placed on or over the coals, which created a more effective heat and left few black marks. One must assume that ancient Egyptian cooks would have been more adept with their fires and that their cooking pots could have easily borne fewer marks than the experimental vessels.

Our experimental cooking fires at Elephantine suggest that black marks do not document how the vessel was used to cook (i.e., by being placed besides or above the heat) so much as how controlled the fire was that it was used to cook in. The interior of our fish fry pan was black and smooth from one day of cooking fish, suggesting that many of our interior black marks might be best understood as cooking residues (Skibo, 2013: 63). Some vessels used in the fire had black marks covering little as approximately 20% of its exterior (Figure 23). If such vessels were broken, up to 80% of the sherds could bear no visual evidence of cooking use, thus appearing to have been unused in cooking if we use blackening patterns as the proxy for cooking activity. If we apply these findings to Figure 21: 49% of the corpus shows interior blackening, probably the result of residues left when whatever the vessel contained was heated. 23.0% show fire marks on the exterior

Figure 22 Experimental cooking fire at Elephantine, May 2019. (photo by author)

surface, likely the result of cooking fires. The remaining 66.3% that show no exterior black marks could themselves belong to vessels that were heated but come from areas of the pot that bear no trace of the fire. While our experiments were not conclusive, they do show that these figures drastically underestimate the mass of vessels employed in cooking, a finding that echoes experimental work done with Minoan cooking pots (Morrison et al., 2015: 122). It is necessary to model cooking fires and their results more carefully. Experimental work provides another key to thinking through ceramic material was used and deposited and the roles and played in private life.

5.6 Conclusion

Collaborative work and cross-material analyses must be the norm when approaching studies of private life. The complexity of lived experience is not bounded by a single material or offer simple, direct equation with identity. Ethnicity is fluid and changeable. Yet, seemingly paradoxically, ethnicity is built on repetitive material practices in both the public and private sphere. Ceramics were integral for display and identity creation as they were key to production and consumption activities. Quantification, contextual analysis vis-

Figure 23 Blackening marks on fish fry pan after three rounds in the
experimental fire, May 2019. (photo by author)

à-vis the assemblage and material from comparative sites, and experimental
archaeology allow us to gain information on vessel role and function, from
which we can extrapolate umbrella issues such as identity. Thus, issues of
ethnicity and food production should be worked in tandem as their results will
reinforce and aid each other.

Much work remains to be done. There is space for more ceramicists, more data,
and more theorizing in the field. For example, it would be useful to compare
ceramic quantitative analyses within and across sites, enabling us to understand
potential ethnic difference throughout the country and into Nubia. A common
nomenclature, sampling strategy, and collection methodology would forward
such an aim and allow data to be easily encoded in databases and made shareable.
Today we must rethink our relationship to data and collection strategies in an
effort to ensure that ceramic data are analyzed and published.

6 Finding People through Potsherds

When holding an Old Kingdom potsherd, one is holding an object manufactured
by an individual as much as 4,500 years ago. Their fingerprints and the marks of
their fingers are sometimes on the vessel. Someone drank beer out of the
container, made an offering with it, paid for labor with it. They reused the pot.

They threw it away. Thinking about how and why pots were made, used, and deposited, requires that we think about Egyptian society, identity, and practices.

This Element showcased how Egyptian ceramics highlight the social complexity of Egyptian society and, by extension, the Egyptian state. Pots challenge the oftentimes elite narrative of Egyptian history. Regionalism, ethnic diversity, social consistency, bottom-up change, and domestic practices are all signaled by the ceramic record as pots were inherent to social practice. The nature of ceramics as fundamental to production, exchange, trade, and domestic life merit ceramic analysis an important place in the toolbox for writing Egyptian social history. They are data that can and should be mined by all who are interested in reconstructing Egyptian society. Thus, ceramic data would best be accessible not only to ceramicists and in ceramic publications. Excellent work on Egyptian ceramics has been and continues to be done, yet it has borne little impact on reconstructions of Egyptian society or social relationships and made little dent in standardized Egyptian history. Still text and monument, pharaoh, and the elite dominate. Clearly, understanding that a study of ceramics can be, and should be, driven by social frameworks is only part of answer. Otherwise, ceramics would always be incorporated into the general dialogue and the questions embraced.

Pottery, however, presents both logistical and epistemological barriers to integrating into broader social research: data recording, time, and publication. Most pottery data are generated during field research and are ultimately published as articles or monographs by ceramicists. Good practices in this production line from fieldwork to publication can potentially lower barriers, allowing for cross-site research and comparison by ceramicists and archaeologists and inclusion of pottery data in studies that are not primarily ceramic or written by ceramicists.

The first issue is data recording during field research. Field programs should consider and include ceramic research from the beginning of their research design to enable optimal ceramic collection and recording processes to be put in place as early in the project as possible. Ceramic data acquisition will last the length of a project, and frequently longer, as artifact recording often moves slowly. Developing an appropriate field methodology for ceramic data collection is itself a huge challenge that absorbs much of a specialist's time. As with any science, the data collected are not guaranteed to answer a given research question. But good collection methodology and recording systems are fundamental, providing the basic data for all future work: directly at the site and comparative; locally, regionally, or nationally scaled. As apparent throughout this Element, quantifiable ceramic data in terms of sherd counts, weights, measurements, and visual assessments are important for assessing vessel function. Accordingly, quantifiable data are key to detailed study revealing agency outside of the royal house, at the regional or local level. Similarly, archaeometry has the potential to yield important data about production and exchange but has been underutilized in Egyptian ceramic studies. Increasing data from petrographic studies, at minimum, would be important to include when a project yields the appropriate material. This work requires money, staff, and time. Without it, the potential of ceramic analysis becomes a moot point.

Publication of the basic ceramic corpus from any field project presents the fundamental ceramic data from the site for study and use by other researchers. Such publications must be data rich and full of illustrations. Fundamental questions, particularly chronology, must be addressed; larger social questions can appear with the basic publication or wait to be addressed in other publications. It is an important step toward data preservation, as archaeology is a destructive science and ceramics are particularly likely to have been (selectively) dumped and discarded after recording. At many Egyptian sites, it is impossible to go back and study the complete body of ceramic material from earlier excavations. Very few places in the world can afford to save every sherd! Currently, an archaeological project's basic ceramic corpora are typically published either as articles in excavation monographs or as stand-alone monographs, both published at the end of the project when data collection is complete. Articles within the project monograph are valuable because they sit in conversation with other data from the field work such as stratigraphy and other finds. Stand-alone ceramic monographs tend to present larger-scale analysis and more pottery drawings while feeling almost entirely self-contained. Smaller articles focused on specific aspects of the corpus also are written and are absolutely important for a broad analysis of the material. Yet it is the basic corpora that are key to future research.

Publications of basic corpora can support or limit future analyses, especially comparative, state-scaled analyses. For those seeking to answer synthetic questions that require data from many sites, data are primarily accessible through basic ceramic publications that lay out ceramic corpora so that other researchers may see the data, work with it, and compare other pots to it. Yet while basic corpora are fundamental and important, they are limited by their paper format, whether a traditional print publication or an e-publication. In articles and monograph format alike, it is only possible to include a selection of the data that has been studied and recorded.

Digital publication of databases has the potential to enable broader, easier data sharing that would enable cross-site work. Such requires that field recording is based in databases. There is no standardized database or collection methodology in either ceramic studies or archaeology writ large and it is likely that any database will be bespoke, at least to a certain level. Projects like Open Context[7] and OCHRE[8] allow for data sharing and, in the case of OCHRE, born-digital archaeological data. Neither, however, answer the needs of ceramicists, and much work continues to be done with paper, Excel, FileMaker, and a myriad of other solutions in the field. Some projects have computer specialists on their teams who develop custom programs for their projects. Digitization is a challenge that requires staff, brainstorming, and computer skills. However, it is a solvable issue, particularly if one develops their digital solutions early in a project. I have used FileMaker as well as a bespoke system called InfoArch, built by the business intelligence company InfoSol. Database organization has been a key part of our field methodologies, with the goal of having all quantifiable ceramic data born digital to enable more powerful search, more robust analysis, and better data sharing.[9]

Instead of publishing a traditional paper monograph, it would be ideal to publish the basic data as a database online, concurrently with articles or a monograph of analysis in more traditional formats. Digital publication of corpora does not mean immediate data sharing. Data must be cleaned and organized. The database must be presented in such a way as to be usable to people not deeply familiar with the material. The strength of digital publication of the ceramic database is that all information might be made accessible for future researchers. Best practices need to be developed and researcher rights protected via copyright, such as through Creative Commons licensing.

Digital ceramic database publication is suggested here not as a substitute for analysis. Indeed, basic publications often includes crucial analyses of cultural divisions within the ceramic corpus (e.g., Rzeuska, 2006: 430–511) or ceramic functional distribution (Wodzińska, 2011). Such work helps us think through the role and use of ceramics and perhaps could be published independently, in tandem with upload of the ceramic database to the Internet. Digital publication of databases would replace only the corpus part of the publication as a means for broad sharing of large-scale, quantified, fundamental ceramic data to support more extended analyses and collaboration. Work on state-level ceramic production and technology (Nordström and Bourriau, 1993) and on milk use and production (Hendrickx et al., 2002) have all arisen from collaboration. State-scaled research on social organization (Seidlmayer, 1990) and economy (Warden, 2014) show the value of basic publications to later researchers. More data could allow for more synthetic, collaborative work.

For ceramics to impact Egyptian social archaeology more greatly and fully rise to its potential to answer big questions about who the Egyptians were and

---

[7] https://opencontext.org/   [8] https://oi.uchicago.edu/research/ochre-data-service

[9] For conversation on database and BI solutions for ceramic analysis, see Limitless BI, episode 5: https://limitlessbi.com/episode-5-leslie-warden-digging-into-the-data/

how they lived, discourse on these topics must change and become interdisciplinary. It is my hope that this Element provides an entry point for how ceramic research may be incorporated into archaeological projects and social interpretations. The field of Egyptian ceramics has much to offer the broader field and as well as public, general narratives of Egyptian history. Collaborative research with different specialists is an important aspect of this. Most of the questions with which this Element engaged can be addressed most strongly when ceramic evidence is put into conversation with other types of material, be it text, art, bioarchaeology, or other artifacts and features. It is too much for any one individual to have mastery over but provides interesting ground for jointly authored studies.

We may also build a support for and interest in the role of ceramic material and social studies by engaging with the interested public. Public presentation requires that we flip the script, placing the questions first and using ceramics as the data, not the focus. When we present the Egyptians as people with lived experiences and diversity of activities and practices, audiences engage. Such approaches are important to fully incorporate ceramics as a fundamental dataset for building the social narrative. Many ceramics await in the sherd yard, the excavation magazine, and the museum basement, and our understanding of Egyptian society can be made better through more such work.

Glossary

Absolute dating: assigning specific years to an archaeological object or deposit. Absolute dating rarely yields a specific date but instead tends to present as date ranges (e.g., 2600–2200 BC). Before 664 BC, absolute dates in Egyptology frequently come from scientific analyses such as ^{14}C.

Attributes: the characteristics of a ceramic vessel, typically including its shape (such as rim and base type), size, surface treatment, fabric, method of manufacture, and decoration.

Body sherds: sherds from the vessel's body, generally uninformative regarding vessel type.

Coefficient of Variation (CV): (standard deviation/sample size) × 100. The CV expresses the amount of variation of an attribute within a corpus. Attributes may vary independently as they are dually dependent upon the ability of the potter who makes the vessel and the needs or desires of the community who requires it.

Diagnostic sherds: sherds from parts of the vessel that indicate form and/or date: portions of rims, bases, handles, and decorated sherds. Sherds from imported vessels or foreign wares, evident due to different fabric, surface treatment, and decoration as compared to Egyptian ceramics, are commonly included in this category.

Fabric: the material of the finished ceramic vessel. Fabric is composed of the matrix, also called groundmass, and inclusions. The vessel's fabric bears a relationship to its paste – the clay as prepared by the potter – though with chemical and compositional changes due to firing.

Formal attributes: attributes linked to vessel shape (morphology).

Hand building: a method of vessel manufacture where the potter does not turn the vessel on the wheel during production, though the potter might employ simple rotation on a mat or within an emplacement. Hand building techniques include paddle-and-anvil, slab- or coil-building, manufacture over a hump, and use of molds. Hand building does not necessarily yield low-quality or low-value vessels. The Predynastic Period, during which all vessels were hand built, was also the period in which Egyptian vessels were the most beautiful and seemingly showcased status.

Inclusions: non-clay material naturally occurring in the clay body.

Levant: a geographic term, synonymous with the eastern Mediterranean.

Paralleling: equating a vessel found at one site to a like ("parallel") vessel at another site, typically based on morphological attributes. To account for variable function and vessel change over space, the most secure parallels are made by looking at material from similar types of sites (for example, comparing one settlement to another) near to the site in question to account for stylistic diffusion. Paralleling may also help establish vessel function.

Petrography: an analysis of a sherd's cross section to determine a fabric's composition. The section is typically 30 µm thick and cut and polished either by the analyst or an outside lab. Sections are then mounted on a glass slide and analyzed under a polarizing light (petrographic) microscope. Petrography can aid in identification of inclusions, clay type, or general firing temperature, forwarding study of clay origin, paste preparation, and manufacture.

Provenience: archaeological find-spot, including specific horizontal and vertical location of the find.

Relative dating: placing events, objects, and people in an early-to-late sequence without necessarily determining the length of time or specific calendrical placement of individual phases.

Seriation: the relative dating of artifacts by charting the popularity of types over time. Popularity trends can be measured in two ways: stylistic/contextual seriation, which accounts for the presence or absence of a form in a context, or frequency seriation, which accounts for quantities within the assemblage. Seriation dating demonstrates variations between assemblages and is not based on single types or individual vessels.

Sherd: a broken piece of pottery; as opposed to "shard," a broken piece of glass.

Slip: a thin layer of watery clay and pigment applied to a potter as a final step before the vessel is finished, considered part of the vessel's surface treatment. Traditional Egyptian slips are red in color, though cream and black slips are also known.

Stratigraphy: two types exist: horizontal and vertical. Horizontal stratigraphy demonstrates changes in use of a landscape over time. Vertical stratigraphy is composed of superimposed layers of deposition and can provide a guide to relative dating following the geological Law of Superposition: all things being equal, the oldest layers (or *strata*) are the lowest and the newest layers the highest.

Style: at its most basic, the way in which something is made, resulting from human choice between options. Style is closely tied to function and technology; it also communicates information. Debate lies in determining what elements of style have cultural meaning, how they convey meaning, and what that cultural meaning is.

Temper: material intentionally added to the clay body by the potter.

Type: in pottery, vessels sharing a group of common attributes, typically grouped into a typology. Archaeological typologies tend to be based on formal attributes (creating devised typologies) while the typologies created by those using the vessels are often categorized by function (creating folk typologies).

Utilitarian: common ceramics produced for functional purposes. Utilitarian ceramics are typically made of coarse fabrics (i.e., fabrics that are chunky and filled with inclusions) and are often poorly finished.

Ware: the combination of manufacture technique, fabric, surface treatment (such as a slip or other finishing techniques), and sometimes form. A good modern example would be Fiesta Ware, easily identifiable based on vessel shape, glaze, and the material of which it is made.

Wheel: in Egypt, an Old Kingdom technological innovation allowing for the introduction of new forms and showcasing of new technical skill. However, the wheel did not dominate Egyptian ceramic manufacture until some point in the Middle Kingdom

References

Adams, W. Y. & Adams, E. W. (1991). *Archaeological Typology and Practical Reality: A Dialectical Approach to Artifact Classification and Sorting.* Cambridge: Cambridge University Press.

Allen, S. (1998). Queen's Ware: Royal Funerary Pottery in the Middle Kingdom. In C. J. Eyre, ed., *Proceedings of the Seventh International Congress of Egyptologists.* Leuven: Peeters, pp. 39–48.

Allen, S. (2006). Miniature and Model Vessels in Ancient Egypt. In M. Bárta, ed., *The Old Kingdom Art and Archaeology.* Prague: Charles University in Prague, pp. 19–24.

Antonaccio, C. M. (2010). (Re)Defining Ethnicity: Culture, Material Culture, and Identity. In S. Hales & T. Hodos, eds., *Material Culture and Social Identities in the Ancient World.* Cambridge: Cambridge University Press, pp. 32–53.

Arias Kytnarová, K. (2014). Ceramic Finds. In J. Krejčí, K. Arias Kytnarová, H. Vymasalová, A. Pokorná, and J. Beneš, eds., *Abusir XXIV: Mastaba of Werkaure, Vol. 1: Tombs AC 26 and AC 32 – Old Kingdom Strata.* Prague: Charles University in Prague, pp. 71–259.

Arias Kytnarová, K., Jirásková, L., & Odler, M. (2019). Old Kingdom Model and Miniature Vessels from Giza." In A. Kahlbacher & E. Priglinger, eds., *Tradition and Transformation in Ancient Egypt.* Vienna: Austrian Academy of Sciences, pp. 15–29.

Arnold, Do., ed. (1981.) *Studien zur altägyptischen Keramik.* Mainz: Philipp von Zabern.

Arnold, Do. (1988a). The Model Pottery. In D. Arnold, ed., *The Pyramid Complex of Senwosret I.* New York: Metropolitan Museum of Art, pp. 83–91.

Arnold, Do. (1988b). The Pottery. In D. Arnold, ed., *The Pyramid of Senwosret I,* New York: Metropolitan Museum of Art, pp. 106–46.

Arnold, Do. & Bourriau, J., eds. (1993). *An Introduction to Ancient Egyptian Pottery.* Mainz: Philipp von Zabern.

Aston, D. A. (2004). *Tell el-Dab'a XII: A Corpus of Late Middle Kingdom and Second Intermediate Period Pottery, Vol. 1–2.* Vienna: Verlag der Österreichischen Akademie der Wissenschaften.

Bader, B. (2001). *Tell el-Dab'a XIII: Typologie und Chronologie der Mergel C-Ton Keramik.* Vienna: Österreichischen Akademie der Wissenschaften.

Bader, B. (2002). A Concise Guide to Marl C-Pottery. *Ägypten und Levante* **12**, **29–54.**

Bader, B. (2010). Processing and Analysis of Ceramic Finds at the Egyptian Site of Tell el-Dab'a/Avaris ("Eves" and Other Strange Animals). In B. Horejs, R. Jung, & P. Pavúk, eds., *Analysing Pottery: Processing – Classification – Publication*. Bratislava: Comenius University in Bratislava, pp. 209–33.

Bader, B. (2012). Sedment. In R. Schiestl & A. Seiler, eds., *Handbook of Pottery of the Egyptian Middle Kingdom, Vol. II: The Regional Volume*. Vienna: Verlag der Österreichischen Akademie der Wissenschaften, pp. 209–35.

Bader, B. (2013). Cultural Mixing in Egyptian Archaeology: The "Hyksos" as a Case Study. *Archaeological Review from Cambridge* **28** (1), **257–86**.

Bader, B. (2016). Quantification as a Means of Functional Analysis: Settlement Pottery of the Late Middle Kingdom at Tell el-Dab'a. In B. Bader, C. M. Knoblauch, & E. C. Köhler, eds., *Vienna 2 – Ancient Egyptian Ceramics in the 21st Century*. Leuven: Peeters, pp. 47–67.

Bader, B. & Ownby, M. F., eds. (2013). *Functional Aspects of Egyptian Ceramics in their Archaeological Context*. Leuven: Peeters.

Bader, B., Knoblauch, C. M., & Köhler, E. C., eds. (2016). *Vienna 2 – Ancient Egyptian Ceramics in the 21st Century*. Leuven: Peeters.

Bagh, T. (2012). Abu Ghalib: Early Middle Kingdom Settlement Pottery from the Western Nile Delta. In R. Schiestl & A. Seiler, eds., *Handbook of Pottery of the Egyptian Middle Kingdom. Vol. II: The Regional Volume*. Vienna: Österreichischen Akademie der Wissenschaften, pp. 13–47.

Baines, J. (1996). Contextualizing Egyptian Representations of Society and Ethnicity. In J. S. Cooper & G. M. Schwartz, eds., *The Study of the Ancient Near East in the Twenty-First Century: The William Foxwell Albright Centennial Conference*. Winona Lake, IN: Eisenbrauns, pp. 339–84.

Baines, J. (2009–10). Modeling the Integration of Elite and Other Social Groups in Old Kingdom Egypt. *Cahier de Recherches de L'Institut de Papyologie et d'Egyptologie de Lille* **28**, **117–44**.

Bárta, M. (1995a). Pottery Inventory and the Beginning of the IVth Dynasty ("Multiplier Effect" in the IVth and the "Law of Diminishing Returns" in the VIth Dynasties. *Göttinger Miszellen* **149**, **15–24**.

Bárta, M. (1995b). Archaeology and Iconography: *bḏȝ* and *ꜥprt* Bread Moulds and "Speisetischzene" Development in the Old Kingdom. *Studien zur Altägyptischen Kultur* **22**, **21–35**.

Bárta, M. (1996). Several Remarks on Beer Jars Found at Abusir. *Cahiers de la céramique égyptienne* **4**, **127–31**.

Bárta, M. (2010). Borderland Dynamics in the Era of the Pyramid Builders of Egypt. In I. W. Zartman, ed., *Understanding Life in the Borderlands:*

Boundaries in Depth and in Motion. Athens, GA: University of Georgia Press, pp. 21–39.

Bats, A. (2017). Archéologie expérimentale à Ayn Soukhna : la production du pain. Accessed October 19, 2019. https://amers.hypotheses.org/560

Bats, A. (2020). The Production of Bread in Conical Moulds at the Beginning of the Egyptian Middle Kingdom. The Contribution of Experimental Archaeology. *Journal of Archaeological Science: Reports* **34, Part A**. https://doi.org/10.1016/j.jasrep.2020.102631

Beeck, L. op de. (2004). Possibilities and Restrictions for the Use of Maidum-Bowls as Chronological Indicators. *Cahiers de la céramique égyptienne* **7, 239–80**.

Bietak, M. (1997). Avaris, Capital of the Hyksos Kingdom: New Results of Excavations. In E. Oren, ed., *The Hyksos: New Historical and Archaeological Perspectives.* Philadelphia, PA: The University Museum of the University of Pennsylvania, pp. 87–139.

Bourriau, J. (1986–87). Cemetery and Settlement Pottery of the Second Intermediate Period to Early New Kingdom. *Bulletin of the Egyptological Seminar* **8, 47–59**.

Bourriau, J. (1990). The Pottery. In P. Lacovara, ed., *Deir el-Ballas: Preliminary Report on the Deir el-Ballas Expedition, 1980–1986.* Winona Lake, IN: Eisenbrauns, pp. 15–22.

Bourriau, J. (1996). The Dolphin Vase from Lisht. In P. der Manuelian, ed., *Studies in Honor of William Kelly Simpson* 1. Boston, MA: Museum of Fine Arts, pp. 101–16.

Bourriau, J. (2007). The Vienna System in Retrospect: How Useful is It? In Z. A. Hawass & J. Richards, eds., *The Archaeology and Art of Ancient Egypt: Essays in Honor of David B. O'Conno*r, Vol. 1. Cairo: SCA Press, pp. 137–44.

Bourriau, J. (2010). *Kom Rabia: The New Kingdom Pottery.* London: EES.

Bourriau, J. & Gallorini, C. (2016). *Survey of Memphis VIII. Kom Rabia: The Middle Kingdom and Second Intermediate Period Pottery.* London: EES.

Bourriau, J., Nicholson, P., & Rose, P. (2000). Pottery. In P. Nicholson & I. Shaw, eds., *Ancient Egyptian Materials and Technology.* Cambridge: Cambridge University Press, pp. 121–47.

Bourriau, J., Bellido, A., Bryan, N., & Robinson, V. (2006). Egyptian Pottery Fabrics: A Comparison between NAA Groupings and the "Vienna System." In E. Czerny, I. Hein, H. Hunger, D. Melman, & A. Schwab, eds., *Timelines: Studies in Honour of Manfred Bietak* 3. Leuven: Peeters, pp. 261–92.

Braekmans, D. & Degryse, P. (2016). Petrography: optical microscopy. In A. M. W. Hunt, ed., *The Oxford Handbook of Ceramic Analysis.* Oxford: Oxford University Press, pp. 233–65.

Braun, E. (2005). Identifying Ethnicity from Prehistoric Pottery in Ancient Egypt and the Southern Levant. In J. Clarke, ed., *Archaeological Perspectives on the Transmission and Transformation of Culture in the Eastern Mediterranean*. Oxford: Oxbow, pp. 140–54.

Braun, E. (2016). Little Pot Who Made Thee? Dost Thou Know Who Made Thee? In B. Bader, C. M. Knoblauch, & E. C. Köhler, eds., *Vienna 2 – Ancient Egyptian Ceramics in the 21ˢᵗ Century*. Leuven: Peeters, pp. 69–84.

Budka, J. (2016). Egyptian Cooking Pots from the Pharaonic Town of Sai Island, Nubia. *Bulletin de liaison de la céramique égyptienne* **26**, 285–95.

Bunbury, J. M., Tavares, A., Pennington, B., & Gonçalves, P. (2017). Development of the Memphite Floodplain: Landscape and Settlement Symbioses in the Egyptian Capital Zone. In H. Willems & J.-M. Dahms, eds., *The Nile: Natural and Cultural Landscape in Egypt*. Bielefeld: Transcript, pp. 71–96.

Bussmann, R. (2014). Scaling the State: Egypt in the third millennium BC. *Archaeology International* **17**, 79–93.

Butzer, K. (1976). *Early Hydraulic Civilization in Egypt: A Study in Cultural Ecology*. Chicago: University of Chicago Press.

Campagno, M. (2014). Patronage and Other Logics of Social Organization in Ancient Egypt during the IIIrd millennium BCE. *Journal of Egyptian History* **7 (1)**, **1–33**.

Cohen-Weinberger, A. & Goren, Y. (2004). Levantine-Egyptian Interactions During the 12th to the 15th Dynasties Based on the Petrography of the Canaanite Pottery from Tell el-Dab'a. *Ägypten und Levante* **14**, **69–100**.

Conkey, M. W. (1990). Introduction. In M. W. Conkey & C. A. Hastorf, eds., *Uses of Style in Archaeology*. Cambridge: Cambridge University Press, pp. 5–17.

Conkey, M. W. & Hastorf, C. A., eds. (1990). *Uses of Style in Archaeology*. Cambridge: Cambridge University Press.

Costin, C. L. (2001). Craft Production Systems. In G. M. Feinman & T. D. Price, eds., *Archaeology at the Millennium: A Sourcebook*. New York: Kluwer/ Plenum, pp. 273–327.

Dee, M. W. (2017). Absolutely Dating Climatic Evidence and the Decline of Old Kingdom Egypt. In F. Höflmayer, ed., *The Late Third Millennium in the Ancient Near East: Chronology, C14, and Climate Change*. Chicago, IL: Oriental Institute, pp. 323–31.

Dee, M., Ramsey, C. B., & Rowland, J. M. (2008). Evaluating the Effectiveness of Radiocarbon Studies of the Old Kingdom. In H. Vymazalová and M. Bárta, eds., *Chronology and Archaeology in Ancient Egypt (the Third Millennium B. C.)*. Prague: Czech Institute of Archaeology, Charles University in Prague, pp. 1–9.

Doherty, S. K. (2015). *The Origins and Use of the Potter's Wheel in Ancient Egypt.* Oxford: Archaeopress.

Eerkens, J. W. (2000). Practice Makes Within 5% of Perfect: visual perception, motor skills, and memory in artifact variation. *Current Anthropology* **41 (4), 663–68.**

Eerkens, J. W. & Bettinger, R. L. (2001). Techniques for Assessing Standardization in Artifact Assemblages: can we scale material variability? *American Antiquity* **66 (3), 493–504.**

Eyre, C. J. (1999). Village Economy in Pharaonic Egypt. In A. K. Bowman & E. Rogan, eds., *Agriculture in Egypt from Pharaonic to Modern Times.* Oxford: Oxford University Press, pp. 33–60.

Eyre, C. J. (2011). Patronage, Power, and Corruption in Pharaonic Egypt. *International Journal of Public Administration* **34 (11), 701–11.**

Faltings, D. (1989). Die Keramik aus den Grabungen an der nördlichen Pyramide des Snofru in Dahschur: Arbeitsbericht über die Kampagnen 1983–1986. *Mitteilungen des Deutschen Archäologischen Instituts Abteilung Kairo* **45, 133–54.**

Faltings, D. (1998). *Die Keramik der Lebensmittelproduktion im Alten Reich: Ikonographie und Archäologie eines Gebrauchsartikels.* Heidelberg: Heidelberger Orientverlag.

Gandon, E., Nonaka, T., Endler, J. A., Coyle, T., & Bootsma, R. J. (2020). Traditional Craftspeople are Not Copycats: Potter Idiosyncrasies in Vessel Morphogenesis. *PLOS One* **15 (9), e0239362.** https://doi.org/10.1371/journal .pone.0239362

Gatto, M. C. (2005). Nubians in Egypt: Survey in the Aswan-Kom Ombo Region. *Sudan & Nubia* **9, 72–75.**

Gatto, M. C. (2014). Cultural Entanglement at the Dawn of the Egyptian History: A View from the Nile First Cataract Region. *Origini: preistoria e protostoria delle civiltà antiche* **36, 93–123.**

Guasch Jané, M. R., Ibern-Gómez, M., Andrés-Lacueva, C., Jáuregui, O., & Lamuela-Raventós, R. M. (2004). Liquid Chromatography with Mass Spectrometry in Tandem Mode Applied for the Identification of Wine Markers in Residues from Ancient Egyptian Vessels. *Analytical Chemistry* **76, 1672–77.**

Hafsaas, H. (2006–07). Pots and People in an Anthropological Perspective: The C-Group People of Lower Nubia. *Cahier de recherches de l'Institut de papyrologie et d'égyptologie de Lille* **26, 163–71.**

Hartung, U. (2001). *Umm el-Qaab 2: Importkeramik aus dem Friedhof U in Abydos (Umm el-Qaab) und die Beziehungen Ägyptens zu Vorderasien im 4. Jahrtausend v. Chr.* Mainz: Philipp von Zabern.

Hays, H. (2011). The Death of the Democratization of the Afterlife. In N. Strudwick & H. Strudwick, eds., *Old Kingdom, New Perspectives: Egyptian Art and Archaeology 2750–2150 BC*. Oxford: Oxbow, pp. 115–30.

Hegmon, M. (1992). Archaeological Research on Style. *Annual Review of Anthropology* **21**, 517–36.

Hendrickx, S. (1989). De grafvelden der Naqada-cultuur in Zuid-Egypte, met bijondere aandacht voor het Naqada III grafveld te Elkab: Interne chronologie en sociale differentiatie. Vol. II: Tabellen en bibliografie. PhD thesis, Katholieke Universiteit, Leuven.

Hendrickx, S. (1996). The Relative Chronology of the Naqada Culture, Problems and Possibilities. In J. Spencer, ed., *Aspects of Early Egypt*. London: British Museum Press, pp. 36–69.

Hendrickx, S. (2006). Predynastic-Early Dynastic Chronology. In D. Warburton, R. Krauss, & E. Hornung, eds., *Ancient Egyptian Chronology*. Leiden: Brill, pp. 55–93.

Hendrickx, S. (2011). Sequence Dating and Predynastic Chronology. In E. Teeter, ed., *Before the Pyramids: The Origins of Egyptian Civilization*. Chicago, IL: University of Chicago Press, pp. 15–16.

Hendrickx, S., Faltings, D., Beeck, L. op de, Raue, D. & Michiel, C. (2002). Milk, Beer and Bread Technology during the Early Dynastic Period. *Mitteilungen des Deutschen Archäologischen Instituts Abteilung Kairo* 58, **277–304**.

Hillier, J. K., Bunbury, J. M., & Graham, A. (2007). Monuments on a Migrating Nile. *Journal of Archaeological Science* **34, 1011–15**.

Hodder, I. (1982). *Symbols in Action: ethnoarchaeological studies of material culture*. Cambridge: Cambridge University Press.

Hodder, I. (2012). *Entangled: An Archaeology of the Relationships between Humans and Things*. Malden: Wiley-Blackwell.

Holmqvist, E. (2016). Handheld Portable Energy-Dispersive X-Ray Fluorescence Spectrometry (pXRF). In A. M. W. Hunt, ed., *The Oxford Handbook of Archaeological Ceramic Analysis*. Oxford: Oxford University Press, pp. 363–81.

Hood, A. (2018). A Brief Look at First- and Second-Dynasty Ceramics and their Chronological Implications. In P. Kopp, ed., *Elephantine XXIV: Funde und Befunde aus der Umgebung des Satettempels. Grabungen 2006–2009*. Wiesbaden: Harrassowitz, pp. 153–74.

Hope, C. A. (2007). Egypt and "Libya" to the End of the Old Kingdom: A View from Dakhleh Oasis. In Z. A. Hawass and J. E. Richards, eds., *The Archaeology and Art of Ancient Egypt: Essays in Honor of David B. O'Connor*, Vol. 1. Cairo: Conseil suprême des antiquités de l'Égypte, pp. 399–415.

Jacquet-Gordon, H. (1981). *A Tentative Typology of Egyptian Bread Moulds*. In Do. Arnold, ed., *Studien zur altägyptischen Keramik*. Mainz: Philipp von Zabern, pp.11–24.

Janssen, J. (1979). The Role of the Temple in the Egyptian Economy during the New Kingdom. In E. Lipiński, ed., *State and Temple Economy in the Ancient Near East. Vol. 2*. Leuven: Departement Oriëntalistiek, pp. 505–15.

Jones, S. (1997). *The Archaeology of Ethnicity: constructing identities in the past and present*. New York: Routledge.

Kaiser, W. (1957). Zur inneren Chronologie der Naqadakultur. *Archaeologia Geographica* **6, 69–77**.

Kaiser, W., Arnold, F., Bommas, M., et al. (1999). Stadt und Tempel von Elephantine: 25./26./27. Grabungsbericht. *Mitteilungen des Deutschen Archäologischen Instituts Abteilung Kairo* **55, 63–236**.

Kaiser, W., Avila, R., Dreyer, G., et al. (1982). Stadt und Tempel von Elephantine: Neunter/Zehnter Grabungsbericht. *Mitteilungen des Deutschen Archäologischen Instituts Abteilung Kairo* **38, 271–344**.

Kemp, B. J. (2006). *Ancient Egypt: Anatomy of a Civilization*. 2nd ed. New York: Routledge.

Khalifa, E. & Abd Elrahim, E. (2020). Identification of Vessel Use and Explanation of Change in Production Techniques from the Old to the Middle Kingdom: Organic Residue Analysis, Fabric and Thermal Characterization of Pot Sherds from Qubbet el-Hawa, Aswan, Egypt. *Archaeometry* **62 (6), 1115–29**.

Kirby, C. J., Orel, S. E., & Smith, S. T. (1998). Preliminary Report on the Survey of Kom el-Hisn, 1996. *Journal of Egyptian Archaeology* **84, 23–43**.

Knapp, A. B. (2014). Mediterranean Archaeology and Ethnicity. In J. McInerney, ed., *A Companion to Ethnicity in the Ancient Mediterranean*. Malden, MA: Blackwell, pp. 34–49.

Köhler, E. C. (1996). Archäologie und Ethnographie. Eine Fallstudie der prädynastischen und frühzeitlichen Töpfereiproduktion von Tell el-Fara'in – Buto. *Cahiers de la céramique égyptienne* **4**, 133–43.

Köhler, E. C. (1997). Socio-economic Aspects of Early Pottery Production in the Nile Delta. *The Bulletin of the Australian Centre for Egyptology* **8, 81–89**.

Köhler, E. C. (2008). Craft and Craft Specialisation: an introduction. In B. Midant-Reyes & Y. Tristant, eds., *Egypt at Its Origins 2: Proceedings of the International Conference "Origin of the State: Predynastic and Early Dynastic Egypt", Toulouse (France), 5th-8th September 2005*. Leuven: Peeters, pp. 3–6.

Köhler, E. C. (2013). Early Dynastic Chronologies. In A. J. Shortland & C. B. Ramsey, eds., *Radiocarbon and the Chronologies of Ancient Egypt*. Oxford: Oxbow Books, pp. 224–34.

Köhler, E. C. (2014a). *Helwan III: Excavations in Operation 4, tombs 1-50*. Rahden/Westf: Leidorf.

Köhler, E. C. (2014b). Of Pots and Myths – Attempting a Comparative Study of Funerary Pottery Assemblages in the Egyptian Nile Valley during the late 4th Millennium BC. In A. Mączyńska, ed., *The Nile Delta as a Centre of Cultural Interactions between Upper Egypt and the Southern Levant in the 4th Millennium BC*. Poznań: Poznań Archaeological Museum, pp. 155–80.

Köhler, E. C., Smythe, J., & Hood, A. (2011). Naqada IIIC-D – The End of Naqada Culture? *Archéo-Nil* **21**, 101–10.

Kopp, P. (2019). Die Keramikformationen der 1. Zwischenzeit und des Mittleren Reiches auf Elephantine. *Bulletin de liaison de la céramique égyptienne* **29**, 243–304.

le Provost, V. (2016). La céramique du début du Moyen Empire à Ayn Asil. Productions locales et importations. In B. Bader, C. M. Knoblauch, & E. C. Köhler, eds., *Vienna 2 – Ancient Egyptian Ceramics in the 21st Century*. Leuven: Peeters, pp. 349–67.

Lehner, M. (1997). *The Complete Pyramids*. London: Thames and Hudson.

Lehner, M. (2000). Fractal House of Pharaoh: Ancient Egypt as a Complex Adaptive System, a Trial Formation. In T. A. Kohler & G. J. Gumerman, eds., *Dynamics in Human and Primate Societies: Agent-Based Modeling of Social and Spatial Processes*. Oxford: Oxford University Press, pp. 275-353.

Longacre, W. A. (1985). Pottery Use-Life among the Kalinga, Northern Luzon, the Philippines. In B. Nelson, ed., *Decoding Prehistoric Ceramics*. Carbondale, IL: SIU Press, pp. 334–46.

Longacre, W. A. (1999). Standardization and Specialization: what's the link? In J. M. Skibo & G. M. Feinman, eds., *Pottery and People*. Salt Lake City, UT: University of Utah Press, pp. 44–58.

Loprieno, A. (1988). *Topos und Mimesis. Zum Ausländer in der ägyptischen Literatur*. Wiesbaden: Harrassowitz.

Manning, J. G. (2013). "Egypt." In P. F. Bang & W. Scheidel, eds., *The Oxford Handbook of the State in the Ancient Near East and Mediterranean*. Oxford: Oxford University Press, pp. 61–93.

Marchand, S. (2017). Remarques sur les moules à pains et les plaques de caisson dans l'Égypte ancienne. *Bulletin de liaison de la céramique égyptienne* **27**, **223–50**.

84   *References*

Marchand, S. & Baud, M. (1996). La céramique miniature d'Abou Rawash. Un dépôt à l'entrée des enclose orientaux. *Bulletin de l'Institut français d'archéologie orientale* **96, 255–88**.

Martinet, É. (2011). *Le nomarque sous l'ancien empire.* Paris: Presses de l'université Paris-Sorbonne.

McCall, G. S. (2018). *Strategies for Quantitative Research: Archaeology by the Numbers.* New York: Routledge.

McGovern, P. E. (1997). "Wine of Egypt's Golden Age: An Archaeochemical Perspective." *Journal of Egyptian Archaeology* **83, 69–108**.

Miroschedji, P. de & Sadeq, M. (2005). The Frontier of Egypt in the Early Bronze Age: Preliminary Soundings at Tell es-Sakan (Gaza strip). In J. Clarke, ed., *Archaeological Perspectives on the Transmission and Transformation of Culture in the Eastern Mediterranean.* Oxford: Oxbow, pp. 155–69.

Moeller, N. (2016). *The Archaeology of Urbanism in Ancient Egypt: From the Predynastic Period to the End of the Middle Kingdom.* Cambridge: Cambridge University Press.

Moreno García, J. C. (1999). *Ḥwt et le milieu rural égyptien du IIIe millénaire: économie, administration et organisation territoriale.* Paris: Champion.

Moreno García, J. C. (2001). L'organisation sociale de l'agriculture dans l'Égypte pharaonique pendant l'ancien empire (2650-2150 avant J.-Chr.). *Journal of the Economic and Social History of the Orient* **44 (4), 411–50**.

Moreno García, J. C. (2013). The "Other" Administration: Patronage, Factions, and Informal Networks of Power in ancient Egypt. In J. C. Moreno García, ed., *Ancient Egyptian Administration.* Leiden: Brill, pp. 1029–65.

Moreno García, J. C. (2017). Topsy-Turvy: Lives and Depictions of Workers in Ancient Egypt. In M. E. Babej, ed., *Yesterday – Tomorrow: A Work in Aspective Realism.* Heidelberg: Kehrer, pp. 135–43.

Moreno García, J. C. (2018). Ethnicity in Ancient Egypt: An Introduction to Key Issues. *Journal of Egyptian History* **11, 1–17**.

Morrison, J. E., Sofianou, C., Brogan, T. M., Alyounis, J., & Mylona, D. (2015). Cooking Up New Perspectives for Late Minoan IB Domestic Activities: An Experimental Approach to Understanding the Possibilities and Probabilities of Using Ancient Cooking Pots. In M. Spataro & A. Villing, eds., *Ceramics, Cuisine, and Culture.* Oxford: Oxbow, 115–24.

Mueller, D. (1975). Some Remarks on Wage Rates in the Middle Kingdom. *Journal of Near Eastern Studies* **34 (4), 249–63**.

Newman, D. (2003). On Borders and Power: A Theoretical Framework. *Journal of Borderland Studies* **18, 13–25**.

Nicholson, P. T. (1995). Construction and Firing of an Experimental Updraught Kiln. In B. J. Kemp, ed., Amarna reports VI. London: The Egypt Exploration Society, pp. 239–78.

Nicholson, P. T. & Patterson, H. L. (1985). Pottery Making in Upper Egypt: An Ethnoarchaeological Study. *World Archaeology* **17, 222–39.**

Nicholson, P. T. & Patterson, H. L. (1989–90). Ceramic Technology in Upper Egypt: A Study of Pottery Firing. *World Archaeology* **21 (1), 71–85.**

Nordström, H.-Å. (2011). The Significance of Pottery Fabrics. In D. Aston, B. Bader, C. Gallorini, P. Nicholson, & S. Buckingham, eds., *Under the Potter's Tree: Studies on Ancient Egypt Presented to Janine Bourriau on the Occasion of her 70th Birthday.* Leuven: Peeters, pp. 723–30.

Nordström, H.-Å & Bourriau, J. (1993). Ceramic Technology: Clays and Fabrics. In Do. Arnold & J. Bourriau, eds., *An Introduction to Ancient Egyptian Pottery.* Mainz: Philipp von Zabern, pp.147_90.

Odler, M. (2017). For the Temples, for the Burial Chambers: Sixth Dynasty Copper Vessel Assemblages. In M. Bárta, M. F. Coppens, & J. Krejčí, eds., *Abusir and Saqqara in the Year 2015.* Prague: Faculty of Arts, Charles University, pp. 293–315.

Orton, C. & M. Hughes. (2013). *Pottery in Archaeology.* 2nd ed. Cambridge: Cambridge University Press.

Ownby, M. F. (2009). Petrographic and Chemical Analyses of Select 4th Dynasty Pottery Fabrics from the Giza Plateau. In T. I. Rzeuska & A. Wodzińska, eds., *Studies on Old Kingdom Pottery.* Warsaw: Neriton, pp. 113–37.

Ownby, M. F. (2011). Through the Looking Glass: The Integration of Scientific, Ceramic, and Archaeological Information. In D. Aston, B. Bader, C. Gallorini, P. Nicholson, & S. Buckingham, eds., *Under the Potter's Tree: Studies on Ancient Egypt Presented to Janine Bourriau on the Occasion of her 70th Birthday.* Leuven: Peeters, pp. 751–67.

Ownby, M. F. (2016). Petrographic Analysis of Egyptian Ceramic Fabrics in the Vienna System. In B. Bader, C. M. Knoblauch, & E. C. Köhler, eds., *Vienna 2 – Ancient Egyptian Ceramics in the 21ˢᵗ Century.* Leuven: Peeters, pp. 459–70.

Papazian, H. (2012). *Domain of Pharaoh: The Structure and Components of the Economy of Old Kingdom Egypt.* Hildesheim: Gebrüder Gerstenberg.

Pelt, W. P. van. (2013). Revising Egypto-Nubian Relations in New Kingdom Lower Nubia: From Egyptianization to Cultural Entanglement. *Cambridge Archaeological Journal* **23, 523–50.**

Petrie, W. M. F. (1892). *Medum.* London: British School of Archaeology in Egypt.

Petrie, W. M. F. (1899). Sequences in Prehistoric Remains. *Journal of the Anthropological Institute* **29, 295–301.**

Petrie, W. M. F. (1901). *Diospolis Parva: the cemeteries of Abadiyeh and Hu 1898–99.* London: Egypt Exploration Fund.

Petrie, W. M. F. (1921). *Corpus of Prehistoric Pottery and Palettes.* London: British School of Archaeology in Egypt.

Petrie, W. M. F. (1953). *Corpus of Proto-Dynastic Pottery.* London: British School of Archaeology in Egypt.

Petrie, W. M. F., Mackay, E., & Wainwright, G. (1910). *Meydum and Memphis III.* London: British School of Archaeology in Egypt.

Raue, D. (2002). Nubians on Elephantine Island. *Sudan & Nubia* **6, 20–24.**

Raue, D. (2008). Who was Who in Elephantine of the Third Millennium BC? *British Museum Studies in Ancient Egypt and Sudan* **9, 1–14.**

Raue, D. (2012). Medja vs. Kerma at the First Cataract – Terminological Problems. In I. Forstner-Müller & P. Rose, eds., *Nubian Pottery from Egyptian Cultural Contexts of the Middle and Early New Kingdom. Proceedings of a Workshop Held at the Austrian Archaeological Institute in Cairo, 1–12 December 2010.* Vienna: Österreicheisches Archäologisches Institut, pp. 49–58.

Raue, D. (2018a). *Elephantine und Nubien vom 4.-2. Jahrtausend v. Chr.,* 2 vols. Berlin: de Gruyter.

Raue, D. (2018b). "Zu den Keramikfunden der Frühdynastischen Zeit und des Alten Reiches." In P. Kopp, ed., *Elephantine XXIV: Funde und Befunde aus der Umgebung des Satettempels.* Wiesbaden: Harrassowitz, pp. 185–236.

Raue, D. (2019). Nubians in Egypt in the 3rd and 2nd Millennium BC. In D. Raue, ed., *Handbook of ancient Nubia, Vol. 1.* Berlin: De Gruyter, pp. 567–88.

Redmount, C. (1995). Ethnicity, Pottery and the Hyksos at Tell el-Maskhuta in the Egyptian Delta. *The Biblical Archaeologist* **58 (4), 182–90.**

Reisner, G. A. & Smith, W. S. (1955). *A History of the Giza Necropolis, Vol. II: The Tomb of Hetepheres the Mother of Cheops.* Cambridge, MA: Harvard University Press.

Rice, P. M. (1987). *Pottery Analysis: A Sourcebook.* Chicago, IL: University of Chicago Press.

Richards, J. (2005). *Society and Death in Ancient Egypt: Mortuary Landscapes of the Middle Kingdom.* Cambridge: Cambridge University Press.

Robins, G. (2000). *The Art of Ancient Egypt.* Cambridge, MA: Harvard University Press.

Roux, V. (2019). *Ceramics and Society: A Technological Approach to Archaeological Assemblages.* Cham: Springer.

Rzepka, S., Hudec, J., Jarmużek, Ł., et al. (2017). From Hyksos Tombs to Late Period Tower Houses: Tell el-Retaba – Seasons 2015–2016. *Ägypten und Levante* **27, 19–86.**

Rzeuska, T. I. (2006). *Saqqara II. Pottery of the Late Old Kingdom: Funerary Pottery and Burial Customs.* Warsaw: Neriton.

Rzeuska, T. I. (2011). Grain, Water, and Wine: Remarks on the Marl A3 Transport-Storage Jars from Middle Kingdom Elephantine. *Cahiers de la céramique égyptienne* **11, 461–530.**

Rzeuska, T. I. (2013). Dinner is Served: Remarks on Middle Kingdom Cooking Pots from Elephantine. In B. Bader & Mary F. Ownby, eds., *Functional Aspects of Egyptian Ceramics in Their Archaeological Context.* Proceedings of a conference held at the McDonald Institute for Archaeological Research, Cambridge, July 24–July 25, 2009. Leuven: Peeters, pp. 73–97.

Rzeuska, T. I. & Ownby, M. (2009). Pottery of the Old Kingdom – Between Chronology and Economy. Remarks on Mixed Clay in the Memphite Region. In T. I. Rzeuska & A. Wodzińska, eds., *Studies on Old Kingdom Pottery.* Warsaw: Neriton, pp. 139–53.

Rzeuska, T. I. & Wodzińska, A., eds. (2009). *Studies on Old Kingdom Pottery.* Warsaw: Neriton.

Schiestl, R. & Seiler, A. (eds). (2012a). *Handbook of the Pottery of the Egyptian Middle Kingdom, Vols. 1-2.* Vienna: Österreischen Akademie der Wissenschaften.

Schiestl, R. & Seiler, A. (2012b). Introduction. In R. Schiestl & A. Seiler, eds., *Handbook of the Pottery of the Egyptian Middle Kingdom, Vol. 1: The Corpus Volume.* Vienna: Österreischen Akademie der Wissenschaften, pp. 25–53.

Schneider, T. (2003). Foreign Egypt: Egyptology and the Concept of Cultural Appropriation. *Ägypten und Levante* **13, 155–61.**

Schneider, T. (2010). Foreigners in Egypt: Archaeological Evidence and Cultural Context. In W. Wendrich, ed., *Egyptian Archaeology.* Malden, MA: Wiley-Blackwell, pp. 141–63.

Schneider, T. (2017). "What is the Past but a Once Material Existence Now Silenced?" The First Intermediate Period from an Epistemological Perspective." In F. Höflmayer, ed., *The Late Third Millennium in the Ancient Near East: Chronology, C14, and Climate Change.* Chicago, IL: Oriental Institute, pp. 311–22.

Schneider, T. & Johnston, C. L. 2020. *The Gift of the Nile? Ancient Egypt and the Environment.* Tucson, AZ: University of Arizona Egyptian Expedition.

Schrader, S. A., Buzon, M. R., & Smith, S. T. (2018). Colonial-Indigene Interaction in Ancient Nubia: An Integrative Analysis of Stress, Diet, and Ceramic Data. *Bioarchaeology of the Near East* **12** (1), **1–32**.

Seidlmayer, S. J. (1990). *Gräberfelder aus dem Übergang vom Alten zum Mittleren Reich. Studien zur Archäologie der Ersten Zwischenzeit.* Heidelberg: Heidelberger Orientverlag.

Seidlmayer, S. J. (1996). "Town and State in the Early Old Kingdom: A view From Elephantine." In J. Spencer, ed., *Aspects of Early Egypt.* London: British Museum Press, pp. 108–74.

Seidlmayer, S. J. (2000). The First Intermediate Period (*c.* 2160–2055). In I. Shaw, ed., *The Oxford History of Ancient Egypt.* Oxford: Oxford University Press, pp. 118–47.

Seidlmayer, S. J. (2006). The Relative Chronology of Dynasty 3. In D. Warburton, R. Krauss, & E. Hornung, eds., *Ancient Egyptian Chronology.* Leiden: Brill, pp. 116–23.

Seidlmayer, S. J. (2007). Prestigegüter im Kontext der Breitenkultur im Ägypten des. 3. und 2. Jahrtausends v. Chr. In B. Hildebrant & C. Veit, eds., *Der Wert der Dinge – Güter im Prestigediskurs: "Formen von Prestige in Kulturen des Altertums" Graduiertenkolleg der DFG an der Ludwig-Maximilians-Universität München.* Munich: Herbert Utz, pp. 309–33.

Seiler, A. (2005). *Tradition & Wandel: die Keramik als Spiegel der Kulturentwicklung Thebens in der Zweiten Zwischenzeit.* Mainz am Rhein: Philipp von Zabern.

Shaw, I., ed. (2000). *The Oxford History of Ancient Egypt.* Oxford: Oxford University Press.

Shepard, A. O. (1956). *Ceramics for the Archaeologist.* Washington, DC: Carnegie Institute of Washington.

Shortland, A. J. & Ramsey, C. B., eds. (2013). *Radiocarbon and the Chronologies of Ancient Egypt.* Oxford: Oxbow Books.

Sinopoli, C. M. (2003). *The Political Economy of Craft Production: Crafting Empire in South India, c. 1350–1650.* Cambridge: Cambridge University Press.

Skibo, J. M. (2013). *Understanding Pottery Function.* New York: Springer.

Smith, S. T. (2003a). Pharaohs, Feasts, and Foreigners: Cooking, Foodways, and Agency on Ancient Egypt's Southern Frontier. In T. L. Bray, ed., *The Archaeology and Politics of Food and Feasting in Early States and Empires.* New York: Kluwer Academic; Plenum, pp. 39–64.

Smith, S. T. (2003b). *Wretched Kush: Ethnic Identities and Boundaries in Egypt's Nubian Empire.* London: Routledge.

Smith, S. T. (2007). Ethnicity and Culture. In T. Wilkinson, ed., *The Egyptian World*. London: Routledge, pp. 218–41.

Smith, S. T. (2014). Nubian and Egyptian Ethnicity. In J. McInerney, ed., *A Companion to Ethnicity in the Ancient Mediterranean*. Malden, MA: Wiley Blackwell, pp. 194–212.

Smith, S. T. (2018). Ethnicity: Constructions of the Self and Other in Ancient Egypt. *Journal of Egyptian History* **11, 113–46**.

Snape, S. (2014). *The Complete Cities of Ancient Egypt*. London: Thames & Hudson.

Soukiassian, G., Wuttmann, M., & Pantalacci, L. (1990). *Balat III. Les ateliers du potiers d'Ayn-Asil*. Cairo: Institut français d'archéologie orientale.

Sowada, K. (2009). *Egypt in the Eastern Mediterranean During the Old Kingdom*. Göttingen: Academic Press Fribourg.

Sterling, S. L. (2004). Social Complexity in Ancient Egypt: functional differentiation as reflected in the distribution of apparently standardized ceramics. PhD thesis, University of Washington.

Sterling, S. L. (2009). Pottery Attributes and How They Reflect Intentionality in Craft Manufacture/Reproduction. In T. I. Rzeuska & A. Wodzińska, eds., *Studies on Old Kingdom Pottery*. Warsaw: Neriton, pp. 155–86.

Sterling, S. L. (2015). The Economic Implications of Patterns of Ceramic Vessel Similarity in Ancient Egypt. In C. Glatz, ed., *Plain Pottery Traditions of the Eastern Mediterranean and Near East: Production, Use, and Social Significance*. Walnut Creek, CA: Left Coast Press, pp. 39–67.

Strudwick, N. (1985). *The Administration of Egypt in the Old Kingdom: The Highest Titles and Their Holders*. London: Keagan Paul International.

Szpakowska, K. M. (2008). *Daily Life in Ancient Egypt: Recreating Lahun*. Malden, MA: Blackwell.

Trigger, B. G. (1993). *Early Civilizations: Ancient Egypt in Context*. Cairo: AUC.

Vereecken, S. (2011). An Old Kingdom Bakery at Sheikh Said South: Preliminary Report on the Pottery Corpus. In N. Strudwick & H. Strudwick, eds., *Old Kingdom, New Perspectives: Egyptian Art and Archaeology 2750–2150 BC*. Oxford: Oxbow Books, pp. 278–85.

Verner, M. (1993). The Discovery of a Potter's Workshop in the Pyramid Complex of Khentkaus at Abusir. *Cahiers de la céramique égyptienne* **3, 55–59**.

Vischak, D. (2015). *Community and Identity in Ancient Egypt: The Old Kingdom Cemetery at Qubbet el-Hawa*. Cambridge: Cambridge University Press.

Warburton, D., Krauss, R., & Hornung, E., eds. (2006). *Ancient Egyptian Chronology*. Leiden: Brill.

Warden, L. A. (2011). The Organization and Oversight of Potters in the Old Kingdom. In M. Bárta, ed., *Abusir and Saqqara in the Year 2010*. Prague: Czech Institute of Egyptology, pp. 800–19.

Warden, L. A. (2013). Ceramics and Status at Meidum's Northern Cemetery. *Mitteilungen des Deutschen Archäologischen Instituts Abteilung Kairo* **69, 227–46.**

Warden, L. A. (2014). *Pottery and Economy in Old Kingdom Egypt*. Leiden: Brill.

Warden, L. A. (2015). Centralized Taxation during the Old Kingdom. In P. der Manuelian & T. Schneider, eds., *Towards a New History for the Egyptian Old Kingdom: Perspectives on the Pyramid Age*. Leiden: Brill, pp. 470–95.

Warden, L. A. (2019). Tying Technology to Social, Economic, and Political Change: The Case of Bread Baking at Elephantine. *American Journal of Archaeology* **123 (1), 1–17.**

Warden, L. A. (2020). Where Did All the Beer Jars Go? In J. Kamrin, M. Bárta, S. Ikram, M. Lehner, & M. Megahed, eds., *Guardian of Ancient Egypt, Studies in Honor of Zahi Hawass, Vol. 4*. Prague: Czech Institute of Egyptology, pp. 1629–41.

Wegner, J. (2007). *The Mortuary Temple of Senwosret III at Abydos*. New Haven, CT: Peabody Museum of Natural History of Yale University.

Wegner, J., Smith, V. E., & Rossel, S. (2000). The Organization of the Temple Nfr-KA of Senwosret III at Abydos. *Ägypten und Levante* **10, 83–125.**

Wengrow, D. (2006). *The Archaeology of Early Egypt: Social Transformations in North-East Africa, 10,000–2650 BC*. Cambridge: Cambridge University Press.

Wilkinson, T. (2002). Reality Versus Ideology: The Evidence for "Asiatics" in Predynastic and Early Dynastic Egypt. In E. C. M. van den Brink & T. E. Levy, eds., *Egypt and the Levant: Interrelations from the 4th through the Early 3rd Millennium BCE*. London: Leicester University Press, pp 514–20.

Wodzińska, A. (2006). White Carinated Bowls (CD 7) from the Giza Plateau Mapping Project: Tentative Typology, Use and Origin. In M. Bárta, F. Coppens, & J. Krečjí, eds., *Abusir and Saqqara in the Year 2005*. Prague: Czech Institute of Egyptology, pp. 403–21.

Wodzińska, A. (2007). Preliminary Report on the Ceramics. In M. Lehner & W. Wetterstrom, eds., *Giza Reports, Vol. 1: Project History, Survey, Ceramics, and Mains Street and Gallery III.4 Operations*. Boston, MA: AERA, pp. 283–324.

Wodzińska, A. (2009). *A Manual of Egyptian Pottery. Vol. 2: Naqada III-Middle Kingdom.* Boston, MA: AERA.

Wodzińska, A. (2011). The Ancient Egypt Research Associates Settlement Site at Giza: The Old Kingdom Ceramic Distribution. In N. Strudwick & H. Strudwick, eds., *Old Kingdom, New Perspectives: Egyptian Art and Archaeology 2750–2150 BC.* Oxford: Oxbow Books, pp. 304–13.

Acknowledgments

So many people have helped bring this text to fruition, even (especially?) after the advent of COVID-19. I owe a huge debt of gratitude to the editors of the *Ancient Egypt in Context* series, Anna Stevens, Gianluca Miniaci, and Juan Carlos Moreno García, for inviting me to write for this Element. It was written largely during a sabbatical year leave from Roanoke College. David S. Anderson, Laurel Bestock, Nick Brown, May Pwint Thair Chu, Rebecca Cook, Martin Odler, Mary Ownby, Nicholas Picardo, Joshua Aaron Roberson, Serena Soterakopoulos, and two anonymous peer reviewers all gave valuable feedback on portions of drafts of the text (or in the case of the peer reviewers, the whole text), helping me think through data, issues, and presentation. Their feedback greatly improved the text. Any errors are, of course, my own.

Permission to reprint figures was given by: David S. Anderson (Figs. 1 and 7); the Ancient Egypt Research Associates (Fig. 3); Josef Wegner (Fig. 10); Pieter Collet (Figs. 11, 13, 16, and 17); Teresa McCracken (Fig. 12); and Stephan Seidlmayer (Fig. 15; note that this figure includes pot drawings originally published by Petrie).

I am grateful to the archaeological projects who have trusted me with their ceramics over the years: the South Abydos Mastabas Project, the South Abydos Project, the Abydos Search for Paleolithic Sites (all three Penn-Yale-IFA), the North Kharga Oasis Survey (AUC), and the Realities of Life (Elephantine Island, DAI). These experiences provided the foundation that built my ceramic thinking and methods. Salima Ikram pushed me down the ceramics path – many, many thanks and much love.

To the KHPP team, a group of amazing people and scholars whom I am privileged to direct: working with you is a joy. The KHPP 2019 ceramics team (Ahmed Helmy Shared, Hazem Helmy Shared, Lamloon Mohammed Zain, Mansour Shafiq, May Pwint Thair Chu, Paul Grill, Samer Mohammed Shaat, Shimaa al-Said Arkoub, and Sobhy Gamal Sobhy) is owed a special debt of gratitude for observing, counting, weighing, and recording every. single. sherd. KHPP, like the projects above, operates under the permission of the Ministry of Tourism and Antiquities, and ultimate debt goes to Dr. Khaled el-Enany, Dr. Mohamed Ismail Khaled, Dr. Nashwa Gaber, and the taftishes of Aswan, Damanhour, Sohag, and Wadi el-Gadid.

Thanks to my research assistants who have helped me break down my assumptions and views: Amanda Lumpkin, Rebecca Cook, Serena Soterakopoulos, Samantha Riggs, Jacob Friedrich, Emma Howard-Woods,

Jessica White, Isabella Moritz, and Janelle Costa. Extra thanks go to Jeffrey Martin of Roanoke College's Fintel Library, who ILL's all the things and never judges if it turns out they were in the building all along.

Nothing gets done when you have a small child without excellent childcare. I am forever grateful to New Vista Montessori School and Sittin' Pretty for everything they do. Thanks and love to my friends for their support and encouragement in all things, without which writing+teaching+childcare+pandemic would almost certainly have done me in: Michal Mingura, Liz Ackley, Rachel Aronin, Adriane Horne, Meredith Meier, Nick Picardo, Hannah Robbins, Karin Saoub, Jon Snow, and Meg Snow. And above all: David and Jeannette, you are simply the best, most supportive family one could wish for. It's done!

Ancient Egypt in Context

Gianluca Miniaci

University of Pisa

Gianluca Miniaci is Associate Professor in Egyptology at the University of Pisa, Honorary Researcher at the Institute of Archaeology, UCL – London, and Chercheur associé at the École Pratique des Hautes Études, Paris. He is currently codirector of the archaeological mission at Zawyet Sultan (Menya, Egypt). His main research interest focuses on the social history and the dynamics of material culture in the Middle Bronze Age Egypt and its interconnections between the Levant, Aegean, and Nubia.

Juan Carlos Moreno García

CNRS, Paris

Juan Carlos Moreno García (PhD in Egyptology, 1995) is a CNRS Senior Researcher at the University of Paris IV-Sorbonne, as well as lecturer on social and economic history of ancient Egypt at the École des Hautes Études en Sciences Sociales (EHESS) in Paris. He has published extensively on the administration, socioeconomic history, and landscape organization of ancient Egypt, usually in a comparative perspective with other civilizations of the ancient world, and has organized several conferences on these topics.

Anna Stevens

University of Cambridge and Monash University

Anna Stevens is a research archaeologist with a particular interest in how material culture and urban space can shed light on the lives of the non-elite in ancient Egypt. She is Senior Research Associate at the McDonald Institute for Archaeological Research and Assistant Director of the Amarna Project (both University of Cambridge).

About the Series

The aim of this Elements series is to offer authoritative but accessible overviews of foundational and emerging topics in the study of ancient Egypt, along with comparative analyses, translated into a language comprehensible to nonspecialists. Its authors will take a step back and connect ancient Egypt to the world around, bringing ancient Egypt to the attention of the broader humanities community and leading Egyptology in new directions.

Cambridge Elements ≡

Ancient Egypt in Context

Elements in the Series

Printed in the United States
by Baker & Taylor Publisher Services